LINCOLN CHRISTIAN COLLEGE

W9-CBU-324

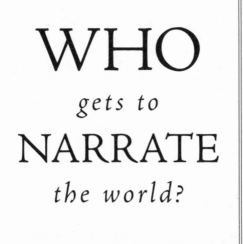

WHO

gets to

NARRATE

the world?

CONTENDING FOR THE CHRISTIAN STORY
IN AN AGE OF RIVALS

ROBERT E. WEBBER

IVP Books

An imprint of InterVarsity Press
Downers Grove, Illinois

InterVarsity Press
P.O. Box 1400, Downers Grove, IL 60515-1426
World Wide Web: www.ivpress.com
E-mail: email@ivpress.com

©2008 by Webber Communications

All rights reserved. No part of this book may be reproduced in any form without written permission from
InterVarsity Press.

InterVarsity Press® is the book-publishing division of InterVarsity Christian Fellowship/USA®, a student movement
active on campus at hundreds of universities, colleges and schools of nursing in the United States of America, and
a member movement of the International Fellowship of Evangelical Students. For information about local and
regional activities, write Public Relations Dept., InterVarsity Christian Fellowship/USA, 6400 Schroeder Rd.,
P.O. Box 7895, Madison, WI 53707-7895, or visit the IVCF website at <www.intervarsity.org>.

All Scripture quotations, unless otherwise indicated, are taken from the Holy Bible, New International Version®.
NIV®. Copyright ©1973, 1978, 1984 by International Bible Society. Used by permission of Zondervan Publishing
House. All rights reserved.

ISBN 978-0-8308-3481-5

Printed in the United States of America ∞

 InterVarsity Press is committed to protecting the environment and to the responsible use of natural
resources. As a member of Green Press Initiative we use recycled paper whenever possible. To learn
more about the Green Press Initiative, visit http://www.greenpressinitiative.org

Library of Congress Cataloging-in-Publication Data

Webber, Robert.
   Who gets to narrate the world? : contending for the Christian story
in an age of rivals/Robert E. Webber
      p. cm.
   Includes bibliographical references and index.
   ISBN 978-0-8308-3481-5 (pbk.: alk. paper)
   1. Apologetics. 2. Christianity and other religions. I. Title.
   BT1103.W43 2008
   269—dc22
                              2008002185

P	19	18	17	16	15	14	13	12	11	10	9	8	7	6	5	4	3	2	1
Y	24	23	22	21	20	19	18	17	16	15	14	13	12	11	10	09	08			

To my wife,

Joanne Lindsell Webber,

for the life and love

we have shared together

119386

Contents

Acknowledgments

If I were to acknowledge all the people, courses, books and events of my life that have influenced the views expressed in this book, it would fill pages. So, I will refer instead to a few situations and people, recognizing without detailing former professors, colleagues and students who have shaped my thought.

Let me first acknowledge the situation that has allowed me time to write. In 2000 I was appointed William R. and Geraldyne B. Myers Professor of Ministry at Northern Seminary in Lombard, Illinois. I deeply appreciate how this endowed chair, with its limited teaching load, has allowed me to spend more time writing.

More specifically, after six years of teaching at Northern Seminary, I was granted a sabbatical of two quarters that stretched from June 2006 to the near end of March 2007. These were months with no teaching or administrative responsibilities, allowing me a long stretch of time to think, read and write. I am keenly aware that I owe Northern Seminary a debt of gratitude for the institutional support they have granted me.

I also want to express a special word of thanks to my editor, Joel Scandrett. Then there is Ashley Gieschen, my administrative assistant. Ashley was with me from the day I started at Northern. I simply could not do what I do without Ashley. She has been gifted with a servant heart, and no one could be more helpful or faithful or supportive than Ashley. She is a coworker in every way, a consultant, a spiritual adviser, a planner, a friend.

In August of 2006 I was diagnosed with pancreatic cancer. I wish to thank my dear wife, Joanne, who immediately gave up all her plans for our sabbatical and became my 24/7 caregiver. Her hands and feet became the hands and feet of Jesus. She nursed me and cared for me, making sure that when I was well enough, I could write unencumbered by other responsibilities. These were the most difficult months of our life together, yet we were gifted with a closeness and spiritual intimacy unparalleled in our marriage. This book simply could not have been written without her and to her the book is dedicated.

Thanks in particular to these people and to the many unnamed others who contributed to my life and thought as reflected in this work.

Introduction

A Wake-Up Call

This book addresses the most pressing spiritual issue of our time: *Who gets to narrate the world?*

At one time the Western world was narrated by the Christian God and the biblical story of his work in Israel and through Jesus to redeem and restore the whole creation. Today, this story of God's cosmic salvation has been lost in the West. In Europe the light has nearly flickered out, and in North America the light is growing dim. New challenges now appear on the horizon.

These new challenges were identified in 2006 in the prologue to "A Call to an Ancient Evangelical Future." The writers state that the North American expression of evangelicalism needs to be especially sensitive to the *new external and internal* challenges facing God's people" (italics added; for the Call see pp. 118-22).

What are the new challenges?

The Call identifies them in the following words: "These external challenges include the current cultural milieu and the resurgence of religious and political ideologies. The internal challenges include evangelical accommodation to civil religion, rationalism, privatism, and pragmatism."

This dual challenge—the threat of Islamic religious nationalism on the one hand and the weakening of Western Christian faith due to cultural accommodation on the other hand—constitute the deep spiritual struggle that this book is all about. How can a weakened Christian faith stand up to the aggressive goals of Islamic nationalism and its desire for religious world domination?

Radical Islam and Christianity are in conflict. Radical Islam, of course, does not represent the majority of Muslims. It is clearly a minority. Most Muslims do not desire to go to war with the West. But Radical Islam has an extremely high profile in the media worldwide and in the Muslim world itself. Besides access to oil money, one of the factors that gives Radical Islam so much power and influence is that many moderate Muslims are not willing to challenge Radical Islam. They remain silent in the face of sometimes violent rhetoric by their fellow Muslims.

While Islam and Christianity have much in common in both heritage and in beliefs, there are many crucial ways in which they disagree. There is much common ground on which to build relationships and on which Muslims and Christians can be, to use Francis Schaeffer's term, cobelligerents in the face of a secular society. Our different views of God, Jesus, Muhammad and the Scriptures, and our differing visions for what God desires to do in the world will mean, however, that in some senses Islam and Christianity always have been and always will be rivals. That, however, is not what I am talking about when I speak of Radical Islam.

When I refer to Radical Islam, I mean Muslims represented by such groups as the Muslim Brotherhood in Egypt, the Jamaat-e-Islami in Pakistan and the Taliban in Afghanistan, these and others often being under the influence of a movement sometimes called Wahhabism or Salafism. Those who follow these teachings often call themselves unitarians. This relatively recent fundamentalist reform movement within Islam dates to the eighteenth century but has grown in influence in the twentieth century.

The external challenge I speak of in this book is from this form of Islam. For Christians it is a spiritual battle. For Radical Islam, the faith of Islam is not primarily spiritual but the external submission to Allah, an acceptance of the teaching of his prophet Muhammad and strict legal obedience to Shari'a law.

Let's look at these two challenges to the Christian faith—the external and the internal—more deeply.

The External Challenge: Radical Islam

The Western world of developed countries is shrinking and dying while the Eastern Muslim world is coming alive and spreading.

The demographic picture. Muslims are growing at a rapid rate and stand ready to become the majority population in many countries. For a society to keep its population the *same*, the norm is 2.1 children per couple. America's birth rate is 2.1, but many other developed nations are not reproducing themselves. Consider these statistics:

Greece:	1.3 births per couple
Italy:	1.2 births per couple
Spain:	1.1 births per couple
Canada:	1.48 births per couple
Europe:	1.38 births per couple
Japan:	1.32 births per couple
Russia:	1.14 births per couple
Muslims:	3.5 births per couple (in the above countries)

Mark Steyn says, "What's happening in the developed world is one of the fastest demographic evolutions in history." He explains:

> Much of what we loosely call the Western world will not survive the twenty-first century, and much of it [the Western world] will effectively disappear within our life times, including many if not most European countries. . . . [I]t's the end of the world as we know it. . . . Islam, however, has serious global ambitions, and it forms the primal, core identity of most of its adherents in the Middle East, South Asia and elsewhere. Islam has youth and will, Europe has age and welfare."[1]

While the developed world of Western civilization is in decline, the Islamic world is experiencing significant growth and now has substantial populations in every developed country. Between 1970 and 2000, the "developed world *declined* from just under 30 percent of the global population to just over 20 percent, and the Muslim nations *increased* about 15 percent to 20 percent."[2]

I have mentioned the demographic challenge because it highlights the spiritual struggle we Christians face. Radical Muslims have spread to countries where Christians have the freedom to worship and evangelize. When such Muslims come to political power, they could force their religion on the entire population, demanding that Christians become Muslim or face persecution. Consider that "of the forty-six Muslim majority nations in the world, only three [are] free."[3] Radical Muslims do not embrace freedom of conscience, nor do they tolerate differences. Of the 1.2 billion Muslims in the world 300 million are committed to Radical Islam, and the numbers grow every day.

Consider what Bernard Lewis, one of the world's most respected historians of Islam has to say in his *New York Times* bestseller *What Went Wrong? The Clash Between Islam and Modernity in the Middle East.*

> Osama bin Laden . . . in February 1998 . . . proclaimed a *jihad* in the name of the "World *Islamic* Front." . . . In this proclamation he called on his followers "to kill Americans and their allies, both civil and military. . . . By God's leave, we call on every Muslim who believes in God and hopes for reward to obey God's command to kill the Americans and plunder their possessions wherever he finds them and whenever he can. Likewise we call on the Muslim ulema and leaders and youth and soldiers to launch attacks against the armies of the American devils and against those who are allied with them from among the helpers of Satan . . . " For those who respond to this call, the conflict is clearly a war to the death between Muslims and unbelievers, the latest phase in a struggle that has been going on for more than fourteen centuries since the time of the Prophet Muhammad, the revelation of the Qur'an, and the advent of Islam. . . .
>
> One can only hope that, in time, the cause of freedom will triumph once again as it has already triumphed over the Nazis and

the Communists. If it does not, the outlook for the Islamic world, and perhaps for the West, will be grim.[4]

The threat of Radical Islam. During the course of writing this book I have shared my concern about Radical Islam with a number of people and have been surprised at how many dismiss the goals of Islamic fundamentalism as a "bump in the road." So let me express my concern about the threat of Radical Islam with one example.

You may remember the furor over Pope Benedict XVI's remarks made at a lecture given at the University of Regensburg in Germany in September 2006. In his speech addressing faith and reason, he quoted the Byzantine emperor Manuel II Palaeologus, who, during a debate with Islam in the Medieval era, said, "Show me just what Mohammed brought that was new, and there you will find things only evil and inhuman, such as his command to spread by the sword the faith he preached."

The emperor spoke the *truth*. Radical Islam is motivated by world conquest. Yes, there are Muslims throughout history and even now who do not openly subscribe to the expansion of their faith through violence, but precious few Muslims are standing up against the Islamic extremists. And world domination—by the sword if necessary—is the theological commitment of Radical Islamic eschatology.

The response to Pope Benedict's comment by Islamic extremists is a case in point. The response to the pope by Al-Qaeda in Iraq was, "This war against Christianity and the West will go on until Islam takes over the world." In a statement addressing the pope the Mujahedin Shura Council, an umbrella organization of Sunni extremists in Iraq, stated "You and the West are doomed, as you can see from your defeat in Iraq, Afghanistan, Chechnya and elsewhere. . . . You infidels and despots, we will continue our Jihad and never stop until God avails us to chop your necks and raise the fluttering banner of monotheism, when God's rule is established governing all people and nations."[5]

Radical Muslims are convinced that they alone worship the one, true

God, who has called them to destroy the infidels so that Allah (which means, *the* God) is properly honored and obeyed throughout his universe. Eventually, Allah will bring the whole world under his command as delivered and interpreted by Muhammad. Then, when the entire world lives under Shari'a law, the world will be at peace.

There is a physical aspect to resistance against Radical Islam. However, my primary concern in this book is not physical warfare but the spiritual battle in which we Christians are to engage. The words of Paul are entirely appropriate: "For our struggle is not against flesh and blood, but against the rulers, against the authorities, against the powers of this dark world, and against the spiritual forces of evil in the heavenly realms" (Eph 6:12). For this reason we must recognize that we are dealing with a deeply grounded spiritual struggle. That is what makes the question of who gets to narrate the world the most pressing spiritual question of our time.

However, there is another side to the question—*the weakening of the church by its cultural accommodation*—and thus the fear that many will wilt in the face of religious persecution.

The Internal Issue: Christian Accommodation to Culture

The challenge of Radical Islam demands that we take inventory of our present understanding and practice of the faith. My conviction—and that of a growing number of Christians—is that the Christian faith in the later part of the twentieth century and now in the twenty-first century has been weakened by its accommodation to culture.

One of the major reasons why the church has fallen prey to a cultural accommodation is that it has become disconnected from its roots in Scripture, in the ancient church and in its heritage through the centuries. This failure of the church to keep faith with its own origins and history is in and of itself a matter of cultural accommodation. For we live in a society that has lost its own heritage. We now drift in a sea of pluralism and relativism with little sense of our past. If it is true that the road to the future lies in the past, it is also true that when the past has been lost or neglected there is no certain future. We are at that point now in Western culture, not only in the broad cultural sense but also in the church which has increasingly followed the lead of culture and lost its connection to the Christian past.

When the past is lost, as it now is in our Western world, there is nothing left to focus on except the self. We live in a culture of disbelief regarding our Christian heritage. However, when it comes to our personal well-being and future, we live in the culture of belief in the *self*. There is almost nothing the self cannot do. So, the popular guru Dr. Phil (without denying that he has some helpful insights) has titled his bestselling book *Self Matters*. His main point is that we must create our own life through the rediscovery of the inner self. If this is so, then our life in this world must be self-generated. There are no objective, common guidelines for the fulfilled life.

Christopher Lasch addresses the focus on self in his well-known book *Culture of Narcissism*, a book I highly recommend. He speaks of "our culture's indifference to the past," which "shades into active hostility and rejection." This indifference has become "the most telling proof of that culture's bankruptcy."[6]

What Lasch says about our cultural situation can be and must be applied to the evaluation of our faith and to the church's heritage. The narcissism that is so prevalent in our worship songs, in our prayers and preaching, and in a misguided spirituality that focuses on the journey of the self is a sign of our impoverished understanding of the gospel and our Christian heritage. One frightening result of narcissism is that "we allow 'experts' to define our needs."

One of the most dangerous groups of experts who have set out to define our needs are the marketers who have successfully managed to turn our culture into a consumerist society. They know how to sell us what we don't need.

Once again Christopher Lasch is on target. He refers to our market-driven consumerist society as the creation of "the propaganda of commodities." After the 1960s, when the new technology began to satisfy "our basic material needs," manufacturers were forced to convince people to buy goods for which they are unaware of any need.[7] To accomplish this need, a new discipline emerged: advertising.

The approach to advertising was "to promote consumption as a way of life." To persuade people to purchase products that would change their lives, the appeal centered on romance—"allusions to exotic places and vivid experiences."[8] Buy this or that product, we were told, and your life will be fulfilled. It will bring new vigor to your life, make you popular, improve your sex life and result in unending happiness. Romance and sex sell.

We can readily see that focusing on fulfillment through owning this product, taking that special vacation, or living in a particular house has caused a shift in values. The value of fulfilling work is no longer in the work itself. Finding meaning in work has been exchanged for working for money. Money buys material things that provide meaning.

Furthermore, instead of dealing with real issues, politics is dominated by advertising and consumption. Those who win elections are not always those with the best qualifications, the finest character or the greatest experience. Instead, elections are obtained by those who can produce the flashiest spectacle that captures the imagination.

The church too has been influenced by current business models, by market-driven advertising and by the spectacular. The consumer model has especially affected worship, which is the true measure of the church. Jesus has become a product to sell, and worship is the primary channel for sales. Most churches do provide more in-depth Christian instruction in small groups and home studies. However, there are a good number of people who never get past the window dressing of worship entertainment, where they continually feed on pabulum rather than the meat of God's Word and the sustenance of communion. The substance of worship—remembering God's saving deeds in the past, culminating in Jesus Christ, and anticipating the overthrow of all evil at Christ's coming—has been lost.

There is much more to be said about these two challenges—Radical

Islam and Christian accommodation to culture. However, I will return to both throughout this book. For I am convinced that the people of God, whose faith has been undermined by cultural accommodation, have not been adequately trained in the spiritual discipline of God's narrative and the Christian heritage of the church. This is what is needed in order to deal with the twin threats of Radical Islam and Western narcissism.

Conclusion

The overriding theme of this book is *to respond to these challenges by understanding and practicing the fullness of God's narrative.* Whether you are a pastor, a youth worker, a worship leader, an evangelist, a teacher or an active layperson in the church, the effect of restoring God's narrative is manifold. It will not only change you and the church, it will invigorate your theological thinking and restore your worship, your spirituality and the church's life and witness in the world.

By understanding and practicing God's narrative in the church, in its ministries and in our personal lives, we may experience a substantial change in society. In the *Letter to Diognetus*, an anonymous second-century document, the writer makes an analogy between the presence of the church in the world and the soul in the body. "What the soul is in the body" the author writes, "Christians are in the world."[9] This analogy reveals that the question, *Who gets to narrate the world?* is essential to the mission of the church and to our personal witness.

This is why I am calling us back to a comprehensive understanding of God's narrative and to a recovery of the cosmic nature of the good news. The Father, Son and Holy Spirit—not Allah or the self—have created the world, have reclaimed and redeemed it, and will ultimately rule over it in the new heavens and new earth. Christians need not only to be able to *say* these words, we need to *demonstrate* what they mean in the present contest with the powers of evil directed against us.

The brevity of this work is intentional. I want it to serve as a wake-up call, a call to the kind of knowledge that leads to deeper spiritual commitment of our life in this world and to spiritual readiness for the struggle that lies ahead.

Knowing that the gates of hell cannot prevail against the church, we must now prepare ourselves by relearning not only God's story in biblical times (chap. 1) but also how God's story was formed in pagan Rome (chap. 2), and how it affected the foundations of Western civilization (chap. 3). We also need to know how the story was lost (chap. 4), to know why secular relativism and pluralism cannot produce the will to survive in our postmodern, post-Christian, neopagan world (chap. 5), to be aware of Radical Islam and other contenders to the faith (chap. 6), and demonstrate to the world how God's story can revive the West, fortify the foundations of civilization, and transform lives and culture as we once again seek to narrate the world Christianly (chap. 7).

Surely, the rediscovery of God's narrative and its implications for ministry are the most pressing spiritual issues facing the church at the beginning of the twenty-first century.

How will the mission of God—which is to be proclaimed and lived out by the church—fare in the twenty-first century in the face of the twin threats of American narcissism and Radical Islam?

Summary

- Christianity and Radical Islam are in conflict—a conflict that will continue to explode into the twenty-first century and rival the Christian faith in the Western world.

- The goal of Radical Islam is religious world domination. The eschatology of Allah is for all to submit to Allah's revelation to Muhammad and live under Shari'a law.

- Western Christianity is in a weakened state due to its cultural accommodation to consumerism, pragmatism, narcissism and other secular ideologies.

- The current challenge to the church and to us as members of the body of Christ is to recover the fullness of God's narrative and the vitality of its life in the world.

Recommended Reading

Huntington, Samuel P. *The Clash of Civilizations and the Remaking of the World Order.* New York: Simon & Shuster, 1996.

Lasch, Christopher. *Culture of Narcissism: American Life in an Age of Diminishing Expectations.* New York: W. W. Norton, 1991.

Steyn, Mark. *America Alone. The End of the World as We Know It.* Washington, D.C.: Regnery, 2006.

Notes

[1]Mark Steyn, *America Alone: The End of the World as We Know It* (Washington, D.C.: Regnery, 2006), pp. xvi, xiii, xix.

[2]Ibid., p. xiv (italics added).

[3]Ibid., p. xvi.

[4]Bernard Lewis, *What Went Wrong? The Clash Between Islam and Modernity in the Middle East* (New York: Perennial, 2002), pp. 163-165.

[5]Lee Keith, "Muslims Rage Against Pope," *Associated Press*, September 18, 2006 <www.nysun .com/article/39865?page_no=2>.

[6]Christopher Lasch, *Culture of Narcissism: American Life in an Age of Diminishing Expectations* (New York: W.W. Norton, 1979), p. xviii.

[7]Ibid., p. 72.

[8]Ibid., pp. 72-73.

[9]Eugene R. Fairweather, ed. and trans., "The So-Called Letter to Diognetus," *Early Christian Fathers*, ed. Cyril Richardson (Philadelphia: Westminster Press, 1953), p. 218.

$$\boxed{1}$$

God's Narrative

My parents were missionaries under the African Inland Mission (AIM). Thus it was in the jungles of Africa that I first heard the good news of God in Jesus Christ.

As far back as I can remember I have always known, sung and loved that great gospel song "Tell me the old, old story, . . . of Jesus and his love." Most Christians love that song because the words take us to the heart of what the Christian faith is all about. However, I wonder if most of us have a *full* grasp of what that story is all about?

Many will say "that story is about Christ who died for *me*, in *my* place, in *my* stead. He paid the price for *my* sin, forgave *me* and now *I* have eternal life." Of course this is true. The personal application of the work of Christ must never be disregarded.

However, there is another side to the old, old story. I didn't hear this side of the gospel from my father, nor did I hear it in college or even seminary. Today this other side of the good news is more commonly known, so perhaps you have heard it.

What I am talking about is the "cosmic" dimension of the gospel. My father read the Bible selectively, as most conservatives did back in the 1930s, 1940s and 1950s. Of course, he read "For God was pleased to have all his fullness dwell in him, and through him to reconcile to himself all things, whether things on earth or things in heaven, by making peace through his blood, shed on the cross" (Col 1:19-20). My guess is that my father's eyes focused on the phrase "His *blood* shed on the cross," but failed to see the phrase "to reconcile to himself all things." That is just the way it is—early evangelicalism focused on the blood shed for *me*, but missed the point of the *cosmic salvation for all things* that resulted from the sacrifice of Christ. I am no exception.

I didn't begin to see the universal nature of God's work in all of history until I was a full-fledged faculty member at Wheaton College. I learned of God's cosmic work in my late thirties, and here I am, nearly forty years later, still unpacking the implications of God's involvement in our history to reverse the human condition, to change the course of history and to rescue not only creatures but all of creation.

It is this creational side of the atonement, this world-encompassing work of Christ that has been lost by many of us and needs to be recovered. Paul captures this cosmic side of God's work when he reminds the Corinthians that "God was reconciling the world to himself in Christ" (2 Cor 5:19). What does this mean? It means that God's story is cosmic, it has to do with the whole world and all of history. This comprehensive vision of God for his whole creation has been plowed beneath our consciousness and lies dormant, waiting to be awakened, to burst forth in our hearts and minds, and shape our culture as well as the future foundations of civilization.

What is that story of God—that story which so desperately needs to be recovered in all its significance and power?

An Introduction to God's Story

First, let me make it clear that I am *not* saying that the average Christian cannot recite the framework of God's story. In Sunday school, preaching, worship and small group Bible studies everyone will recognize the creation; the Fall; the patriarchs; Moses and Israel; the prophets; the incarnation, life, death and resurrection of Jesus, and the new heavens and the earth as the pieces of the story.

What I am saying is that the *fullness* of God's story is lost. As with a puzzle, there is too much concentration on this or that piece without seeing the whole picture.

God's story suffers from reductionism and privatism. The failure to put the whole biblical picture together is a result of the cultural accommodationism identified in the introduction. Specifically, it is the problem of reductionism. The Christian faith has been reduced to a few doctrines of self-interest. In my own background, my dad and his pastor friends concentrated almost exclusively on five doctrines: sin, sacrificial atonement, conversion, sanctification and premillennialism. What was missing was a thoroughgoing connection between creation, incarnation and the re-creative acts of God (such as the resurrection and restoration of creation). My dad, though a devoted Christian and a passionate preacher, lost the fullness of the Christian story because he created a story around five pieces of the puzzle instead of the whole picture. The Christian faith was reduced to the problem of *my* sin, the work of Christ for *me*, the necessity of *my* conversion and the expectation of *my* faithfulness to live like a Christian. *I* was made the center of the story. *I* needed to invite Jesus into *my* life and *my* journey so he would walk with *me* and bless *my* life and *my* ministry.

God calls us to his story. By contrast, the original story, the one delivered by the apostles to their successors in the early church, was not nearly so much *my* narrative as it was God's. And God speaks his narrative through the Bible. God's story is about the *whole* world from its very beginning to the very end. It includes all the nations and governments of the world; it includes the earth, sun and sky; it includes the entire universe. This story even includes you. God, the divine narrator, is saying: I have a purpose for humanity and a purpose for creation and history. I am not asking for permission to join your narrative (although I do); *I am asking you to join my narrative of the world, of human existence, and of all history.*

What is that narrative?

The Great Fullness of God's Story

The fullness of God's story is captured in the three words—*creation, incarnation, re-creation*. At first it may seem that these words represent three doctrines, and consequently a kind of reductionism similar to my father's. Not so—these words constitute a connecting symbol for the whole story of God. Let me tell you that story.

The centrality of Christ in God's story. First, Christ connects everything. He is the Alpha and Omega. For example, I was traveling on a plane from San Francisco to Los Angeles a few years ago. I was sitting next to the window, reading a Christian book. The man next to me, obviously from the Eastern hemisphere, asked, "Are you a religious man?" "Well, yes," I said. "I am too," he responded. We began talking about religion. In the middle of the conversation I asked, "Can you give me a one-liner that captures the essence of your faith?" "Well, yes," he said. "We are all part of the problem, and we are all part of the solution."

> CHRIST CONNECTS EVERYTHING. HE IS THE ALPHA AND OMEGA.

We talked about his one-liner, a statement I felt was very helpful. After a while I said, "Would you like a one-liner that captures the Christian faith?"

"Sure," he responded.

"We are all part of the problem, but there is only one man who is the solution. His name is *Jesus*."

The point I made is very biblical and any Christian would readily agree with it. Jesus is the central figure of the Christian faith. He is the one who *reverses the entire human situation.* The first Adam plunged the human race into rebellion against God. Humanity has made a mess of this world (not only human beings, but the whole world), so God became incarnate, uniting himself to humanity, so that God himself in perfect union with humanity could reverse the human plight caused by Adam and perpetuated by every one of us. So God in Christ not only rescues us, he rescues the whole creation. This truth is clearly taught by Paul: "For since death came through a man, the resurrection of the dead comes also through a man. For as in Adam all die, so in Christ all will be made alive" (1 Cor 15:21-22; see also Rom 5:12-21).

These words remind me of my favorite line in Mel Gibson's *The Passion of the Christ*. Jesus is carrying the cross to Golgotha and falls. A shadow appears, so we know a person is there, but we are not sure who it is. We are led to believe it is his mother. Jesus looks up at her, his face covered with dirt and blood, his body tense from the ordeal of his beatings, sweat gleaming off his body, and with hope in his eyes says, "I make all things new." Here is the narrative in its fullness. The world and its history belongs to God, and he has been, is now, and will be making all things new. The triune God has become involved in history in order to win back his creation.

The triune nature of God's story. Many Muslims consider the Christian understanding of the triune God to be a heresy. They charge Christians with polytheism, the belief in many gods. For this reason it is imperative that Christians understand what we mean when we confess God to be triune.

I went to a Christian college that faithfully adhered to the *triune nature of the Godhead*. However, theology, including the doctrine of the Trinity, was "proven" through a rationalistic, proof-oriented method. Proof for the Trinity was based on the inerrant foundation, the Bible. The method used to arrive at a triune conviction was analytical. It consisted of listing all the verses of the Bible that referred to God the Father as God, Jesus as God and the Holy Spirit as God. "See," it was proclaimed, "God is triune."

I remember feeling uneasy about this analysis and somewhat guilty that my response was, "Is that all there is?" and "So what?" The whole exercise felt futile to me and caused me to think that doctrine arises out of a logical analysis of Scripture. No one asked me to look for the mystery of the triune God at work in the history of the world from beginning to end.

It wasn't until I began to study the early church fathers that I began to see that God is not static but dynamic. The static view of God is a Greek notion. God, so to speak, "sits in the heavens." But the God of the Bible is a triune God of action. God the Creator acts in history and becomes incarnate as a man to rescue the entire created order.

The ancient church fathers follow this narrative approach: The Son reveals the Father and the Spirit. They see God's redemptive work in cosmic history as the united work of the Father, Son and Holy Spirit. The entire Godhead is at work in creating the universe; in establishing a covenant relationship with Israel; in the life, death and resurrection of Jesus Christ; in the birth and history of the church; and in the final outcome of history. This is why the Nicene Creed (A.D. 325) affirms that Jesus is of the same essence as the Father (a view that Muslims find repugnant) and is the living Word of God, through whom everything was made. The Creed confesses that Word to be

> eternally begotten of the Father, God from God, Light from Light, true God from true God, begotten not made, of one Being with the Father. Through him all things were made. For us and our salvation he came down from heaven; by the power of the Holy Spirit he became incarnate from the Virgin Mary, and was made man. For our sake he was crucified under Pontius Pilate. . . . On the third day he rose again.

Jesus reveals God as triune and active! For example, in the matter of creation, the Nicene Creed confesses the Father as the "maker of heaven and earth," the Son as the one "through [whom] all things were made," and the Holy Spirit as "the Lord, the giver of life." The creed ends with "we look for the resurrection of the dead and the life of the world to come." The triune God is active in his entire story—the story of creation, resurrection and the life to come.

The Historical Nature of God's Story

Creation. The story of the biblical God really begins in the Godhead, the

Trinity. God is no static monad but a community of persons united in being and love. This God, so filled with love, longs to have others join his community. He made creatures and creation to share in his own community of Father, Son and Spirit. This is not a "spiritualized" story but one that is worked out in history with real people—not all of them very nice or pious—and in real events. A quick overview of this story as it is happening in time, space and history will help us understand how real it is.

We understand creation in the light of God's love. God creates a world to be a *habitation for himself* and brings into being a people in his image to enjoy *communion with him* and to unfold culture and civilization *to his glory*. The Genesis description of the Garden is one of peace, tranquility, relationship and work. God and humanity enjoy communion with each other as humanity cares for the Garden as the theater of God's majestic creativity.

Fall. However, *evil enters the picture*. Evil is not simply the absence of good, nor is it merely erroneous choice. Evil is revolt, disobedience, resistance. It is a human (and demonic) refusal to carry out God's purposes in history. It is a deliberate, intentional and violent rejection of God. It is a choice to unfold culture away from God under a submission to the enemy of God, Satan, the father of all that is sin, destruction and death in the world.

Good and evil are in *conflict*. This conflict is seen in all of history, from the beginning to the end. However, central to the conflict is God's promise to Satan:

> I will put enmity
>   between you and the woman,
>   and between your offspring and hers;
> he will crush your head,
>   and you will strike his heel. (Gen 3:15)

God's goal in history, so to speak, is to win back his world by his own two hands—the incarnate Word and the Holy Spirit—and to unite humanity with the community of God. His original creational purpose will be fulfilled at the end of history.

However, evil and death, which are the consequences of sin, now *reign* in all creation. The dark tide of evil and death envelopes all creatures, all creation, all culture-making, all cities and all of civilization. Humanity is paralyzed in a condition of alienation from God, from each other and from ourselves. A dehumanizing of self and others extends into all human cultures. Genesis 3–6 describes this frightening and violent human and cultural situation. It also presents God's response—"The LORD was grieved that he had made man, . . . and his heart was filled with pain" (Gen 6:6). In the biblical narrative, God responds with the flood and the salvation of Noah and his family, and the human race gets a new start.

God then begins to establish a particular people of his own to live in *communion and obedience* to him, *to form a culture and influence civilization* according to his purposes.

- In Abraham God called a family into being.

- In Isaac God established a tribe.

- In Israel God formed a nation.

- In David God established a kingdom.

- In Jesus God called forth the people of God, the church.

Israel is a *unique nation* called to be a sign of the coming Messiah and the victory of God over all evil. Consider the foreshadowing symbolism of Israel. Israel's history is full of types or metaphors for spiritual truths:

- *The people of Israel suffering in bondage* is a type of the suffering of all humanity separated from God.

- *Moses* is an early symbolic vision of Christ, the one who comes to the suffering world to liberate it from sin and suffering, and to redeem it.

- The *exodus event* is an early type of the Christ event, bringing redemption and release from the oppressor.

- *The prophets, priests and kings* are also early glimpses of Christ as God's eternal prophet priest and king.

- *The law* reveals the character of Christ who models what a human being, made in the image of God, was meant to be.

- *The tabernacle* is a visual image of the incarnation, of the word made flesh who "tabernacled" among us and made God's glory present.

- *The burned sacrifices* offered symbolize the sacrifice of Christ, who gave himself as a propitiation for our sins.

- *The holiness of the sabbath day* is a reminder of the resurrection, the new beginning of creation, the eternal rest of God in the new heavens and the new earth.

- *The Passover festival* reminds us that Christ is our Passover.

- *The hope of Israel* to exist in a world of peace, where the lamb will lie down with the lion, represents the Christian eschatology and ultimate hope where the peace (*shalom*) of God will rest over the entire created order.

Israel, both past and present, is a visible, tangible, community of people on earth that gives a living witness to the reality of the God who is involved with his creation. Within creation, in God's people, there is always a witness of God initiating a relationship. God reaches out to his creation, longing to bring about the Garden—a place of his habitation, a loving people doing his will. But God's people always fail—again and again. God sends the prophets to call them to return. But God's people do not listen.

Incarnation. Then, in the fullness of time, God himself becomes incarnate. The Word is made flesh. God, so to speak, becomes earthbound. The Word becoming incarnate is much more than God stepping into history. In the incarnation God literally becomes his creation. He assumes the creation as the eternal Alpha and Omega—the great "I Am"—actually "becomes," "takes on," and "receives into himself" the material world that he alone created. In the incarnation, there is a perfect joining of heaven and earth, the human and the divine. This union takes place, as stated by the Council of Chalcedon (A.D. 451):

without confusion, without change, without division, without separation; the distinction of the natures being in no way annulled by the union, but rather the characteristics of each nature being preserved and coming together to form one person and one subsistence.[1]

In other words, God, the divine, is united with all creation in Jesus Christ so that, as we popularly state, Jesus is 100 percent divine and 100 percent human (wholly God and wholly human). The redemption of the world is brought about by God as the *man* who represents all humanity—and his name is Jesus.

But why this incarnation? Why is God united to his own creation and creatures? The New Testament speaks of this union as the great mystery of God revealed in Jesus Christ. The mystery is the mystery of reconciliation, of rescue, of the reversal of the enmity between God and humanity.

Humanity, as I have already indicated, has rebelled against God's purposes, not only personally but also in respect to the God-given task to unfold creation after God's purposes. Men and women are in a horrible situation. There is nothing we can do to repair our relationship with God. We are bent toward living in rebellion against God. The only hope for humanity is in God. Only God can come to our rescue. Only God can restore the Garden.

But God chooses to restore humanity not by a decree of reconciliation, not by a sentimental forgiveness, not by a soft love, but by entering into union with humanity. *In Jesus, God comes in human skin to reverse the human condition and reconcile humanity to the Father.*

> GOD, THE DIVINE,
> IS UNITED WITH ALL
> CREATION IN
> JESUS CHRIST.

The reversal of the human plight of separation between God and humanity already began when Mary, called of God to bear the Christ, responded to the angel's announcement "May it be to me as you have said" (Lk 1:38). In those words the reversal of sin began. From the moment of conception, the child conceived in the womb of the virgin Mary began to reverse the revolt of Adam and his entire posterity.

In his humanity as Jesus, God took into himself the rebellion of the first Adam and the consequence of his sin, which was death for us all. Not only was the decomposition of the human body taken into the humanity of Jesus but also the death that hung over all the earth, all culture-making, all cities and civilization. The violence that proceeds from the human heart and extends into the political, economic, institutional, familial and personal life of us all was received in the human body of Jesus. For he who was without sin was made sin for us all.

In his short life of thirty-three years Jesus continued to reverse the effects of sin on every stage of human life—infancy, adolescence, adulthood. He showed to all the life that God intended for his original creation. There on the hills of Palestine, by the sea, in the synagogue, he demonstrated what life looks like for a human being who is in full communion with God.

Yet he came to do more than show us this life. He came to be that very life, to lift humanity into his own humanity and do for us what we are unable to do for ourselves. He came to enter our suffering. He came to be damned for us all so that he may become chosen for us all. He was rejected, crucified for our sake, so that his life might be in ours and our life in his. Nailed to the cross of his own creation, he took into his own body and into his divine being the suffering and alienation of all humanity, reconciling God to humanity and humanity to God. He who held heaven and earth in his hands now hung suspended between heaven and earth. On the hard wood of the cross he stretched forth his hands of love in a saving embrace of all.

Jesus' cry "My God, my God, why have you forsaken me?" was the anguished cry of the God-man, and the community of God's being received into itself the fracturing of creatures and creation. The violent rebellion of humanity against God's purposes for the world was taken up into God himself. It was the cry of metaphysical anguish as death struck at the heart of God.

In that moment

- The divine Trinity experienced the human suffering of all people, of all time, of all history.

- The Father and Spirit experienced the death of the Son.

- Death, which is the consequence for sin, wrapped itself like a cloak around the Son of God and made him, who knew no sin, to take into his own physical body and spiritual being, the consequence of sin—death itself.

- The Son embraced the eternal separation of hell itself.

- God himself was wounded in the very essence of his being. He experienced for us our own rebellion, taking it and its consequence into himself in order to overcome and defeat it by his love. As the apostle Paul says, "Death has been swallowed up in victory" (1 Cor 15:54).

There is a great ancient prayer that summarizes God's immeasurable work of redemption. It begins with the words "we adore the life-giving cross" and then cites the reasons why we love that old rugged cross. For

it was there Christ renewed the nature of humanity,
it was there Christ restored the way to heaven,
it was there Christ did away with the penalty of the tree of
   disobedience,
it was there Christ broke the bonds of death,
it was there Christ destroyed the gates of hell,
it was there Christ annihilated the kingdom of death,
it was there Christ freed the human race,
Glory be to thee, O Lord!
Christ then descended into hell.

There is a powerful icon that stands by the pulpit of many Orthodox churches. In this icon we contemplate Christ with his foot firmly planted on the fallen gates of hell. His arm reaches forth into hell. We can hear him cry, "I've defeated Satan and all the powers and principalities of the air. I am the victor over sin and death. Come forth!" And the graves gave up their dead.

Re-creation. Then Jesus, who had tasted death for us all who deserved death, was resurrected to new life, that we too might be raised to newness of life.

The resurrection is a new beginning, a new Garden.

The union with God that humans lost in the original Garden is now restored.

The first Adam had brought sin, death and condemnation.

Jesus, our brother, the second Adam, now reverses the sin of the first humans and brings us righteousness, life and justification.

Humanity is invited to enjoy communion with the Father through the Son, by the Spirit.

Now God and all creation are reconciled.

The promise of the Garden has been made new.

Forty days after his resurrection, our Lord ascended into the heavens with a shout—the shout of victory.

The powers of evil were now in chains that restrict their movement and are dragged through the streets.

The angels, the archangels, the cherubim, the seraphim and the whole heavenly host gather to greet the Christ, the Victor, who has crushed the head of the seed of the serpent, and is now seated on the throne. And

> every creature in heaven and on earth and under the earth and on
> the sea, and all that is in them, [exclaim]
>> "To him who sits on the throne and to the Lamb
>> be praise and honor and glory and power,
>>> for ever and ever!" (Rev 5:13)

And this one, this Jesus, the incarnate Word of God, the one who reversed the human condition and did for us what we cannot do for ourselves, is our eternal Liturgist. He stands always before the Father, interceding for those for whom he died and was raised again.

Now, he reigns from the heavens. The earth is his footstool, and when all his enemies have been put down for good (they are conquered now, but not yet submissive), he will come again to reign over all creation. Every knee shall bow and every tongue confess "Jesus is Lord," and the Garden of the new heavens and the new earth will become the place of eternal bliss.

Conclusion

I have summarized the narrative of God. This is the narrative that Christians confess. The church witnesses to this story: we sing it in our worship, proclaim it in our speech and preaching, inhabit it in our spirituality, live it in our relationships, enact it through works of love, and extend it in missions throughout the world.

There is no story, no philosophy, no religion, no ideology in all of heaven and earth that is a more profound narrative of the world. That God, who is the Creator, would himself become the Redeemer is unthinkable. But it's true. God takes our death and suffering into himself and defeats it on the cross. He reclaims his universe when he rises from the dead to conquer evil and restore the Garden.

All other stories of the world—whether Muslim extremism or American individualism—are stories of humanity living under the demand of a God who expects each person to make themselves acceptable through a system of works. Works righteousness always says, "We are part of the problem. We are also part of the solution." Grace always says, "There is one person who is the solution. His name is Jesus."

I have combed through books on the theological story of Islam looking for a God who would suffer on our behalf, a God of reconciliation, a God who renews the face of the earth. But what I find is a God of demand, a God who is limited to a revelation of words—the final, ultimate inerrant words to Muhammad. Allah demands that the whole world come under these words and be in obedience to Shari'a law. This God of Islam expects true believers to spread his word and his rule throughout the whole world and bring all nations and all people under his rule.

The Islamic story is the story of humanity living under the demand of a God who expects each person to make him- or herself acceptable through a system of works. The Christian story is one of God's grace extended to all humanity because "God so loved us, that he gave his only begotten son." God himself reverses sin and conquers death to restore the entire creation. What a story!

But I have also lived my life as an American and an evangelical, and cut my teeth on the narrative of the rugged American individual. I have watched in recent years as the more noble features of that story—hard work, self-sacrifice, personal integrity—have given way to laziness, greed and narcissism. The narrative that once made America great has become the narrative that is leading our society—and the church along with it—into a downward spiral of self-indulgence, which has weakened our faith and stunted our souls.

> THERE IS ONE
> PERSON WHO IS
> THE SOLUTION.
> HIS NAME IS JESUS.

We may be at war with Islamic extremists, and that war has its place. But the ultimate battle with Radical Islam is not physical. It is a clash of spiritual narratives. And that spiritual battle has two fronts. While we are battling Radical Islam, we are also in a struggle for the soul of the church in America, a struggle between God's narrative, with God at the center, and my narrative, with the self at the center. The narrative of American narcissism tells us that nothing is more important than the self. By contrast, God's narrative tells us that we will only become what we are meant to be when we submit ourselves to his story.

Whose God rules over our lives? Whose God rules over history? Whose God will rule over all creation forever?

We Christians had better be ready to give the reason for the hope that lies within.

It is not evidence, or logic or philosophy.

It is the narrative.

God's narrative.

All of it—in its fullness.

Summary

- Jesus is Lord of the universe, not just *my* life.

- The incarnation is the missing key in evangelical thought. The incarnate Word does not merely "step into history." The Word becomes humanity, time, space and history to rescue creatures and creation.

- Evangelical reductionism focuses on the sacrificial nature of the atonement without adequate emphasis on the victory of Christ over the powers of evil (*Christus victor*).

- Islam has no way to deal with the powers of evil—other than a God who demands physical death to all who will not submit to Allah's authority and live under Shari'a law.

- There is no story in all the universe comparable to the narrative of the biblical God who enters our suffering and death to overcome it and win back his creation. It is a story worth dying for.

- God's narrative must be recovered in its *fullness*, especially considering the American insistence on individualism and the Muslim claim to world domination.

Recommended Reading

Aulén, Gustaf. *Christus Victor*. New York: Collier, 1968.

Notes

[1]*The Book of Common Prayer* (New York: Seabury Press, 1979), p. 864.

2

God's Narrative Emerges in a Pagan Roman World

I have become convinced from my own experience and from talking with friends and former students that most of us don't remember much from the courses we took in college, maybe not even in graduate school.

For example, I would be hard put to list the courses I took in college, let alone remember the specific content or even the teacher's name! Nevertheless the total impact of education does play an important role in who and what we become.

It so happens that I do remember the teachers and textbooks of several courses I took in graduate school. These courses had a profound effect on my thinking and on my formation as a teacher and writer.

One of the courses was on Roman history and society. What I learned in this course was the political, religious, philosophical and moral setting of the Roman Empire. The second study was on the apostolic fathers of the church, the immediate successors to the apostles.

In my pre-graduate-school days I followed the fairly typical Protestant sequence of jumping from New Testament times to the sixteenth century Reformation. My historical chronology was Paul, Augustine (fifth century), Aquinas (thirteenth century), Luther, Calvin and Menno Simons (sixteenth century). It was as though nothing important happened in the church until the Reformation.

It was an eye-opener for me to read the actual writings of the second century, such as the *Didache* (*The Teaching of the Twelve Apostles*), Ignatius (bishop of Antioch, A.D. 110), Justin Martyr (first Christian apologist, A.D. 150), and Irenaeus (bishop of Lyon, A.D. 180, the most important theologian of the second century, who defended Christianity against the Gnostics).

Finally, I had found the link that made the connection between the apostles and the early church. I also found the link between the early church and the Reformation. I discovered that the apostolic fathers and other ancient fathers of the church who lived and wrote between the third and sixth century had also shaped the sixteenth-century Reformers.

What I loved about these two courses is that they gave me both the cultural context in which God's story was first articulated and a clear insight into the fullness of the story that narrated the world Christianly. These courses made me realize how we need to recover the ancient Christian narrative. That narrative, first developed by the apostles and their immediate successors, takes us to a dependable source for the rediscovery of God's enduring narrative.

> WE NEED TO RECOVER THE ANCIENT CHRISTIAN NARRATIVE.

These courses were also important to me because they introduced me to the social setting of Rome and to the discovery of how Roman society bears a strong similarity to the social setting of our present world. (I will develop the similarity of the present social setting to the Roman society in chap. 6.) For this reason, how Christians narrated the world in the Roman era is applicable to the way we are to narrate God's story today. Let's quickly look at these two issues: the culture of the Roman world, and how Christians narrated the world in that setting. These two issues constitute the topics of this chapter.

The Culture of the Roman World

Students of the ancient era tell us that the Roman world was astonishing in its grandeur and beauty, but it also was a place of unspeakable horror and pain. Jesus was born into the Roman world during the reign of Augustus, the grand nephew of Julius Caesar. Augustus became the emperor at age eighteen and ruled Rome for forty-one years (27 B.C.- A.D. 14). Under Augustus the Roman world prospered and expanded throughout the world. Temples were restored, new cities were established, massive buildings were erected, lavish spectacles were introduced and ancient festivals were revived. For the next two hundred years Rome continued to expand, to extend its rule everywhere, establishing an era of unprecedented peace and prosperity.

However, woven into the fabric of that era of peace and prosperity, Roman culture was rotting at its very center. Because of its decadence, Roman society was falling apart from the inside.

Paul captures the already crumbling reality of the great Roman world in his opening chapter to the Roman Christians. He uses the powerful phrase "God gave them over" three times. Outwardly we see the beauty of this strange, powerful city of one of the greatest civilizations of human history, but Paul knows exactly what is going on inwardly in the hearts and minds of those who live there. Because they do not glorify God,

> God *gave them over* in the sinful desires of their hearts to sexual impurity. . . . They exchanged the truth for a lie, and worshiped and served created things rather than the Creator. . . . Because of this, *God gave them over* to shameful lusts. [And they] exchanged natural relations for unnatural ones. . . . Furthermore, since they did not think it worthwhile to retain the knowledge of God, *he gave them over* to a depraved mind. . . . They have become filled with every kind of wickedness, evil, greed and depravity. (Rom 1:24-26, 28-29, emphasis added).

Paul knew the reality of Rome!

Life for many was harsh, especially under the successors to Augustus—

Tiberius, Nero, Trajan, Hadrian Diocletian and Marcus Aurelius. These despots ruled with a firm hand, cruelly treating all who dared oppose them, including the Christians who were persecuted under their cold hand. The cruelty of Rome is symbolized by the punishment delivered to thieves, murderers, political enemies, Christians and other unfortunates in the great Coliseum of Rome. Here the pagans cheered and laughed as they were torn to shreds by powerful beasts.

One of my personal heroes is Ignatius, the second-century bishop of Antioch and a martyr. At this time Christians were not being systematically persecuted. However, Rome occasionally captured a well-known Christian leader and turned him or her into a martyr as an example to discourage others from becoming Christian. Of course the opposite happened. Every time someone was martyred, the Christian movement grew. Tertullian (A.D. 200) captured the growth resulting from martyrdom in his famous words, "The blood of the martyrs is the seed of the church."

Ignatius was taken by force from Antioch and led in chains to the city of Rome, where (we believe) he was martyred (c. A.D. 107) in the Coliseum (there is no record). En route he wrote seven short letters to the bishops of the cities he passed through, including Ephesus, Smyrna and Philadelphia. He wrote also to the Roman church about his impending martyrdom:

> I am corresponding with all the churches and bidding them all realize that *I am voluntarily dying for God*—if, that is, you do not interfere. I plead with you, do not do me an unseasonable kindness. *Let me be fodder for wild beasts—that is how I can get to God.* I am God's wheat and I am being ground by the teeth of wild beasts to make a *pure loaf* for Christ. I would rather that you fawn on the beasts so that they may be my tomb and no scrap of my body be left. Thus, when I have fallen asleep, I shall be a burden to no one. *Then I shall be a real disciple* of Jesus Christ when the world sees my body no more. Pray Christ for me that *by these means I may become*

God's sacrifice. I do not give you orders like Peter and Paul. They were apostles: I am a convict. They were at liberty: I am still a slave. But if I suffer, I shall be emancipated by Jesus Christ; and united to him, I shall rise to freedom.[1]

Life in Rome was cheap. People who got out of hand were treated brutally, and the Romans openly enjoyed the floggings, tortures, burnings and massive killing of those who dared to oppose the Roman Empire.

During the reign of Marcus Aurelius (A.D. 161-180) a turning point occurred that moved the Roman era away from its long period of peace and prosperity. War had broken out in Germany and Persia. Unfortunately many Roman soldiers caught a severe plague, and when they returned home, an epidemic spread throughout the Roman Empire, taking as many as two thousand lives a day. Political leaders decided the scourge came from the Roman gods, who were offended by the presence of Christians. Consequently, the government turned against the Christians and systematically attempted to rid the empire of them in order to recover the gods' favor.

Over the following century or more, Christians lived under the constant threat of persecution. However by A.D. 312 the emperor Constantine converted to Christianity, and by 380 Christianity became the official religion of the Roman Empire. Then, in A.D. 410, the Visigoths invaded Rome. Over the next two hundred years the Roman Empire, once so grand, crumbled into complete rubble. During these years of the failing empire Christians provided the only stability in Rome. The work and witness of Christians during the waning years of the Rome Empire prepared the way for Christians to narrate the world. But before addressing the impact of the Christian narrative, we must return to the first two centuries of the Christian era to understand how Christians emerged triumphant. What kind of life did they live? How did they function in a world of moral decadence, philosophical relativism and religious pluralism?

A culture of moral decadence. Roman culture, like the culture of

Greece before it, embraced a broad range of sexual activity. Christians had to forge their moral narrative in the context of an amoral society—a society very much like our own.

Premarital sex between men and women was taken for granted, even though women were expected to remain virgins until marriage. Adultery was equally common even though Romans frowned on adulterous women.

Homosexuality was common and socially accepted. Some writers of the time do refer to homosexual relations as a disease, and others see it as a birth defect. However, among many writers, the homosexual lifestyle was idealized—especially among philosophers, some of whom went so far as to extol homosexual love between men and boys, teacher and student.

Sex was also a common expectation of certain cultic worship acts. Cults posted rules about the worship of certain gods through sex. In some cults, clients were expected to fast from sexual activity with their wife or other women—married or unmarried—for a day or two before experiencing religious sex.

Because there were no universally accepted absolutes regarding marriage, abortion, adultery or homosexual relations, sexual activity was regulated for the most part by self-interest. The moral decadence of Rome was fertile soil for the countercultural vision of Christian values. These values were not only taught by Christians, they were lived out as a witness to how the divine narrative changes lives.

A culture of philosophical relativism. The Roman world was characterized by many different philosophical convictions—those of Sophists, Socrates, Plato, Aristotle, Cynics, Stoics, Epicureans and many other lesser known views. Also scattered throughout the cities were self-contained pockets of Jews. Christians constantly bumped up against these views and had to narrate their worldview in the context of these conflicting narratives.

The Greek culture, which Rome conquered, was shaped by the Sophists, and there were many Sophists in the Roman era. Accord-

ing to them truth could not be discovered. Consequently they argued
that truth does not exist, and if it did, it wouldn't be possible to know
it. Because there is no knowledge, human beings must take things into
their own hands and live a wise, measured life (much like the secular
humanism of our day).

A new school of thought, first led by Socrates and then his student
Plato, emerged to question the Sophist rejection of universal truth. Socrates was convinced that one must discover what is right and act on that
basis and no other. If humans are the measure of all things, Socrates believed they could agree on a principle that is wrong, which would lead to
disaster. But how could one distinguish right from wrong? Socrates' pupil
Plato answered the question and became the dominant philosopher of
the Roman world.

Plato taught the existence of universal ideals. In his teaching he argued
for a world outside of the visible world we live in. The visible world, he
taught, is but a shadow of the invisible world, which is the real world.
Our souls, he argued, come from this other world and take up residence
in material bodies. Because our souls bear the imprint of universals from
the real world, we can, through philosophical reflection, learn truth and
know right from wrong.

Reason brings us to truth, according to Plato. Reason, the logos or divine word, is actually embedded in the created order. Because universals
are part of an absolute mind, human beings are able, through the use of
reason, to understand the rational design of universals and come to truth,
knowing right from wrong.

The widespread embrace of Platonic philosophy was fertile soil for the
Christian teaching that God's Word, the Logos, had become incarnate
to redeem creation. However, the Greek concept of logos, or universal
reason, was differentiated from the Christian understanding of the Logos
of God as his eternal, incarnate Word. In Jesus Christ, God's essence, his
own wisdom and reason, became incarnate. Jesus is the display of truth, a
living embodiment of the right way to live. Truth is not abstract, it is real,
concrete, right there before your very eyes.

A culture of religious pluralism. The Roman world was a *pagan* world. However, pagans were not, as is often popularly believed, irreligious. The Greeks had twelve Olympian gods. National and city festivals were often held in honor of the gods. In Athens, for example, as many as 120 days of the year were devoted to festive activities for this or that god. (Paul spoke to the Athenians about the "Unknown God" in Acts 17.) There were many private religions as well, especially the mystery cults, which had special rites of initiation. Witchcraft and the occult also attracted many people to a darker side of religion.

Augustus, the emperor of Rome during the birth of Christ, strengthened rule over Rome by establishing the temple of Apollo. Apollo was a god of colonization and culture, and Augustus initiated a long period of peace and prosperity for Rome (27 B.C.-A.D. 14). Swearing fidelity to the Roman emperor as a god became the one religious absolute for all who lived in Rome. A person could worship many other gods, be involved in the mystery religions and the cults, or be totally irreligious. It didn't matter. What mattered was that they acknowledged the emperor as god.

Christians, however, knew that the Lord alone was God. Their refusal to affirm Caesar as a god was viewed by the Roman government as an act of sedition, and Christians were occasionally persecuted for refusing to acknowledge Caesar's divinity.

How Christians Narrated the World
in the Roman Cultural Setting

My brief comments about ancient Rome show that from the very beginning the Christian narrative had to be expressed within a particular cultural setting. The narrative was first applied to the Hebrew communities and then to the Gentiles. It will help us as we think about living in God's narrative to see how Christians narrated the world as it bumped up against the moral relativism, the philosophical uncertainty and the religious pluralism of the Roman world.

Narrating morality in a world of moral relativism. If Jesus Christ is the incarnate Word of God, then he is the one in whom the meaning of the whole world is found. He is the one to whom we go for moral teaching and example.

The new Hebrew Christians were aware of and followed the moral teaching of the Old Testament. But Greco-Roman pagans had little or no access to God's instructions for living. They looked to human wisdom to provide ethical direction, and used rational reflection to seek eternal ideas to guide their knowledge of right and wrong. Yet none of this was sufficient to overcome the moral decadence of pagan culture.

Christians, though, proclaimed moral absolutes in a morally decadent society. They declared Jesus to be God incarnate and proclaimed he had fulfilled all the commands of God in his own person. He lived, they proclaimed, a life of perfection. Therefore, it is in

> JESUS HIMSELF
> IS OUR ETHIC.

Jesus' life, the early Christians argued, that we see what humanity was created to be. For God in Christ, who became one of us for our salvation, also became one of us to model what true humanity looks like. Jesus himself is our ethic. We are to follow him, to do what he did.

This is a great message. But how do we effectively communicate the ethic of Jesus in a pagan world of moral relativism? The early Christians adapted a process originally developed by the Jews to bring Gentile converts to Judaism. They used extended times of instruction and rites of passage. Records show that this method of Christian formation was universally practiced by the churches in the Roman Empire.

What Christians developed—following the Jewish precedent—was a process of initiation into the Christian life, known as the catechumenate (which means "instruction"). Catechism, which had as its aim becoming a follower of Jesus, included stages of conversion, discipleship and spiritual formation. The process culminated in baptism, and then as a follow-up the new Christians concentrated on the meaning of baptism and the Eucharist for Christian living.

Beyond basic Christian character, the catechism included a strong emphasis on caring for the poor, widows, orphans and others in distress. It formed Christians as a counterculture community and resulted in a radical break with the pagan way of life. New Christians were taught to live in moral purity, to be faithful in marriage, to esteem life in the womb and to preserve castaway children. They became servants to all regardless of race or creed. They narrated a life that imitated the life of Jesus.

Narrating faith in a world of philosophical relativism. The Christian faith is not a philosophy in the same way that we think of the philosophies of Socrates, Plato and Aristotle. However, Christianity addresses the same issues—Is there a God? Where did we come from? Does life have meaning? How should we live? What is the destiny of the world and of humanity?

But Christianity approaches these questions in an entirely different manner from philosophy. Philosophy answers these questions from a human perspective. What do the wisest and smartest people think about life? And of course, all the philosophers differ—considerably.

From the very beginning Christians claimed that the answers to these questions are not derived from human speculation but from *revelation*. God initiates a relationship with humanity. Humans only interpret God's actions and words—and that interpretation is not a philosophy but a narrative that discloses the truth about life.

So, where do we find this narrative? In brief, the ancient Christians believed that the truth about life is found in the story of Israel, Jesus and the church. It spread like this:

1. God's story—found in the history of Israel and culminated in the incarnation, death and resurrection of Jesus—immediately formed a new community.

2. This community was initially formed in Jerusalem and, following Pentecost, spread to cities throughout the Roman Empire. These people gathered to remember God's saving action in Jesus Christ. They did this in worship—through sermons that summarized God's work in history and in meals that recollected the Last Supper.

3. When the early Christians gathered in these assemblies, the apos-

tles of Jesus interpreted the life and ministry of Jesus and the events surrounding his death and resurrection. They always interpreted Jesus as the fulfillment of the story of Israel.

4. These stories—of God, the Garden of Eden, Abraham, Moses, the exodus, the wilderness wanderings, the history of Israel, David, the prophets, the psalms and the Promised Land—found their fulfillment in Jesus.

5. The stories of Jesus were remembered in conversation and repeatedly told. His baptism, his temptation in the wilderness, his selection of disciples, his itinerant ministry, his struggles with the Pharisees, the events of Palm Sunday, the betrayal in the garden, his scourging, his last words on the cross, the resurrection and postresurrection meetings with the disciples, his ascension and the coming of the Holy Spirit were all interpreted as the fulfillment of promises made to Israel. These events constituted the narrative of the world!

6. His followers, acting on his final words—the Great Commission—went everywhere telling others the good news of God's reign over all things through Jesus.

7. New Christian communities (churches) were born, and they retold the Christian narrative in new settings.

8. The apostles wrote down their memories in books that came to be known as Gospels—good news books. These books constituted the authoritative texts of the church's beginnings and of the common apostolic interpretation of Jesus' person, work and ministry. They are revered as sacred texts.

9. The churches throughout the Roman world grew, and the apostles sent letters to the churches. The Gospels and these letters were assembled. The apostles died, and their successors read and studied the apostolic memoirs when they assembled for worship.

This great story, born in history, first communicated in preaching and in a meal, was preserved as the various books and epistles were gathered

into one book, the Bible—an authoritative record and explanation of the
one true story of the world delivered by the apostles, who were there at
the original event. The story did not need to be defended by philosophy or any other discipline—it had become a world narrative that people
assembled to hear and enact in their worship. It answered all the main
questions about the origin, meaning and destiny of life. People's lives were
shaped by this narrative, which was proclaimed and enacted in worship.
And the church grew.

Narrating the uniqueness of Jesus in a world of religious pluralism.
From the very beginning of the Christian era, the Christian faith did
not set itself up as one more religious option alongside others. The earliest Christian creed was "Jesus is Lord." This confession immediately set
Christians against all the religions of the Roman world. It was not possible, for example, to be a Christian and to placate the god of agriculture
or festivity.

More important, Christians were immediately at odds with emperor
worship. It was not possible to say "Caesar is Lord" and "Jesus is Lord." If
Jesus is Lord, he is Lord of all creation, Lord over all religions, Lord over
all governments and emperors. Records show that when seekers (this is
what they were called) enrolled in the catechumenate process, the first
question asked them was, Do you renounce all false worship? This declaration was made publicly, in front of the assembly, prior to being admit-
ted into the catechism and beginning the process of being conformed to
the image of Christ. Because of this declaration (i.e., renouncing all false
worship), the rumor spread that Christians were atheists and subversive
anarchists bent on overthrowing the Roman government. For this reason
they were persecuted.

To defend Christians from these accusations, Justin Martyr wrote
The First Apology. This work, the Christian narrative, was addressed to
the emperor, and the government in general, to explain Christian confession and behavior. Justin drew from the prophecies of the Hebrew faith
to show how Jesus is the fulfillment of Israel's hopes. He explains how
the death and resurrection of Jesus is for the salvation of all, how Chris-

tian worship remembers God's saving acts in history culminating in the death and resurrection of Jesus, anticipating his return. Justin argued that Christians are the best citizens of Rome:

> Those who once rejoiced in fornication now delight in continence alone; those who made use of magic arts have dedicated themselves to the good and unbegotten God; we who once took most pleasure in the means of increasing our wealth and property now bring what we have into a common fund and share with everyone in need; we who hated and killed one another and would not associate with men of different tribes because of [their different] customs, now after the manifestation of Christ live together and pray for our enemies and try to persuade those who unjustly hate us, so that they, living according to the fair commands of Christ, may share with us the good hope of receiving the same things [that we will] from God, the master of all. So that this may not seem to be sophistry, I think fit before giving our demonstration to recall a few of the teaching which have come from Christ himself. It is for you then, as mighty emperors, to examine whether we have been taught and do teach these things truly. His sayings were short and concise, for he has no sophist, but his word was the power of God.[2]

In sum, Christians in the Roman world found themselves in a cultural setting of moral decadence, philosophical relativism and religious pluralism. However, they narrated the world in a *new* way. They did not accommodate the faith to culture but set forth the faith in a countercultural way. In a world that had no set beliefs they proclaimed, "We believe." In a world that had no ethic, they proclaimed, "We behave." In a world where there was no belonging, they declared, "We belong."

The Christian Faith Challenged by the Gnostic Heresy

The early church not only faced these external challenges of the Roman culture—immorality, philosophical relativism and religious pluralism—it also faced an enormously popular internal heretical movement known as Gnosticism. Interestingly, we face a new gnosticism today, a kind of resurrection of the old perversion of the Christian narrative. (I will deal with twenty-first-century gnosticism and its threat to the Christian narrative in chapter seven.)

It was in the course on the early church fathers that I first heard of Gnosticism. (The word *gnosis* means "knowledge" and refers to the claim by Gnostic leaders that they had received a *secret* tradition of truth through the apostles, who handed down the *real* truth about Jesus to a few special people.) In the second century Irenaeus, the most important theologian of that time, devastated the Gnostics' arguments in his work *Against Heresies.*

Ancient Gnosticism may be described as a mix of Christian themes with other philosophical and religious ideas of the Roman world. Gnostics generally argued that there were two gods: the god of the material world and the god of the spiritual world. These gods, they claimed, were in eternal conflict. According to the Gnostics the first god was the creator god, the god of the Jews and the Old Testament. Since the created order was regarded by Gnostics as evil and inferior, the creator god was also evil, inferior. Gnostics rejected the body as essentially evil and inferior. Because of this conviction, Gnostics were strongly anti-Semitic and rejected the Old Testament.

On the other hand the good god, according to the Gnostics, is the spirit god from whom all souls derive. The soul, they argued, is imprisoned within the body and subject to bodily appetites, fleshly longings, bad habits and the like. This imprisonment is the basic human problem. Salvation is accomplished when the soul is freed from its attachment to material things, and ultimately to its bodily imprisonment. The soul transcends the body when it is fully enlightened by the *secret* tradition passed down by Jesus.

Many Gnostics believed that Jesus was sent as an emanation from the spirit god. Being an emanation, Jesus did not have a bodily form. According to the Gnostics, he was an appearance of the spiritual god but he was not incarnated in the flesh. The Gnostic Jesus' message was that through the *knowledge* (gnosis) that he possessed, the soul could eventually become free from its physical confinement and escape this world altogether. Enlightenment comes when a person acknowledges the body-soul dualism, awakes to the imprisonment of his or her soul in the body, and achieves the freedom of the soul through acceptance of Jesus' message, as interpreted by Gnostic leaders. Jesus is the guru who shows the way to this enlightenment, much like he is for gnostic New Agers today.

This message resulted in two very different ethics among the Gnostic Christians. There were those who believed the only way to be free from material reality was to live a very ascetic life. They refused to marry or to engage in any pleasures in life, including good food, leisure and sex. The other group believed that because the material world—and therefore the body—did not matter, then a life of debauchery was appropriate because it denied the very existence of the material life. It was common for this second group to feast, hold orgies and otherwise live it up.

> WE FACE A NEW
> GNOSTICISM TODAY.

The broad influence of Gnosticism was defeated by the orthodox claim, championed by Irenaeus, that God's truth had been handed down through apostolic teaching—which was public, not secret—and in the apostles' letters (the Bible), which were accepted as inspired by God, revered in Christian communities and summarized in the Rule of Faith. The Rule of Faith was an early Christian creed, the forerunner of the Apostles' Creed, which served as a summary of God's narrative of the world.

Conclusion

In this chapter I have given you a glimpse of the Roman world in which the faith first emerged.

I have always been struck, and continue to this day to be impressed by, the parallels between the Roman world and our present secular world. Of course I am not saying they are exactly the same. That would be impossible considering the nearly two-thousand years separating us. But the similarities are striking.

The Roman culture was in decline—a place of moral, philosophical and religious relativism and pluralism. Society was ripe for a new, comprehensive narrative of the world. The Christian narrative came, so to speak, at the right time and the right place. I have been asking myself, now, for more than thirty years, *Isn't our Western world in a similar condition and place?*

This leads to my second set of questions, Will we be able to recover the content of the ancient Christian narrative? Will we be able to plant the seed of God's narrative in the spiritually parched ground of today's Western culture and see it thrive once again?

It is discouraging to view the statistics of Muslim growth around the world and especially in the West. It is also discouraging to see how far removed our culture is from Christian influence, and how today's gnostic views have spread to those seeking spiritual direction in this culture. Finally, it is discouraging to see how "lite" the Christian faith in the West has become through its accommodation to our secular culture.

However, in the face of all these discouraging realities, in the early church we have a model of faith that stood up against the moral decay, philosophical relativism and religious pluralism of the day. It did not succumb to its surrounding culture. It called people to a new way of life, to godliness and holiness, to a firm faith in the cosmic Christ who redeems the whole world, and to truth and absolutes. People flocked to this good news.

Could the phenomenon of Christian growth and influence in the early church be repeated today? Or will Radical Islam overrun the Western world by birth and the sword? The countercultural message of the early church challenges us to recover God's narrative: to be bold and fearless in proclaiming truth over against both the violence of Radical Islam and the complacency of the Western Church.

Rodney Stark, author of *The Rise of Christianity*, asks how an obscure, marginalized Jesus movement became the dominant religious force in the West in only a few centuries. We could rephrase his question and ask: How did the Christian faith narrate the world in Roman times? What did that church look like? What did it do to cause such a change in civilization?

In a few centuries Christianity became the official religion of the Roman Empire. And when the empire fell, Christianity influenced the foundations of Western civilization and created a culture that was, until recently, dominant. How did this faith come to establish the narrative structure of the Western world? That is the topic of the chapter three.

Summary

- There are strong similarities between the culture of Rome in its declining years and the current culture of the Western world.

- The moral decadence of today's Western world rivals the moral decadence of the Roman world.

- Although the philosophies current in today's postmodern world differ from the popular philosophies of the Roman world, they have one characteristic in common—absolute relativism.

- The Roman world was highly religious, as is today's world. Religious pluralism is embraced and celebrated today just as it was two thousand years ago.

- Christianity faced the Roman world not with a faith that accommodated itself to their decadence, relativism and pluralism, but with the firm absolutes of God's narrative. People were hungry for truth and readily embraced a countercultural Christianity.

- Christians today must recover the radical nature of the fullness of God's narrative—for God's comprehensive cosmic narrative alone will endure against the Radical Islamic goal of world domination by Allah and Shari'a law.

Recommended Reading

Fox, Robin Lane. *Pagans and Christians.* New York: HarperCollins, 1988.

MacMullen, Ramsay, and Eugene N. Lane, eds. *Paganism and Christianity. 100-425 c.e.* Minneapolis: Fortress Press, 1992.

Notes

[1]Cyril Richardson, ed. and trans., "Letters of Ignatius: Romans," in *Early Christian Fathers,* ed. Cyril Richardson (Philadelphia: Westminster Press, 1953), p. 104.

[2]Edward Rochie Harly, ed. and trans., "First Apology of Justin," in *Early Christian Fathers,* ed. Cyril Richardson (Philadelphia: Westminster Press, 1953).

3

God's Narrative Influences the Foundations of Western Civilization

In the 1960s I enrolled in a graduate school course called "Bibliography and Historiography of Historical Theology." This course ended up changing the direction of my academic career. I had no idea what it was about, but it fit my schedule. So, like a typical student, I thought, *I'll take it and get my credits.*

More than anything else the course was about the interpretation and writing of history. Each of us was to choose a philosopher of history, study his or her work, discuss what we had learned in class, and write a paper. I chose Arnold Toynbee, who had recently published an eight-volume work on the *Study of History.* I was fascinated by his approach. In brief he argued that there are twenty-seven known civilizations in the world, and each followed a cycle moving from birth to infancy, adolescence, maturity and finally to decay and demise. There are some exceptions—a civilization, for example that stops the growth cycle and remains frozen in one stage (e.g., Eskimos). However, the majority of civilizations have traveled the same cycle and display common characteristics in each stage. I quickly began to apply these cyclical principles to the fall of Rome and to the subsequent rise of the church out of the ashes of that remarkable civilization.

Emperor Constantine (c. A.D. 280-337) was a key figure in shifting Rome toward a Christian society. Scholars disagree on the importance of Constantine's conversion. For example, I attended a conference on Constantine's influence some time ago where the first speaker, a Lutheran, began with the words "The best thing that ever happened to the church was the conversion of Constantine." The next speaker, an Anabaptist, began with the words "The worst thing that ever happened to the church was the conversion of Constantine." Needless to say it was an interesting and heated conference.

In this chapter we will look more closely at the fall of Rome and the rise of Christianity. Hopefully, we will glean some insights to help us in our current spiritual struggle with the beliefs of Radical Islam and the secular West.

The Fall of Rome

Regardless of what one thinks of Constantine, his conversion to the Christian faith in A.D. 312 ultimately led to the triumph of Christianity over paganism in the Roman Empire. Constantine's conversion was crucial to the establishment of Christianity in the Roman world, but by no means was it the only factor. Paganism was simply a weak and ineffective religion in the face of the chaos and turmoil of the fourth, fifth and sixth centuries of the Christian era. On the other hand, Christians *rose to the occasion* and won the hearts and minds of the people because of the way they lived out the message of Christ during those years when Rome fell into disarray and collapse.

It is generally conceded that the decline of Rome began in the devastating epidemics of the second and third centuries, when nearly one out of every three Romans died. During the fourth and fifth centuries the Roman Empire was constantly bombarded by plagues, wars and earthquakes, which eroded the once powerful and proud society. In A.D. 410 the Visigoths sacked Rome and destroyed its political infrastructure and civilization. By A.D. 600 Rome was in rubble. In the three hundred years between Constantine and the full collapse of Rome, a Christian society began to emerge.

Two trends are clearly at work in the Christianization of society. First, paganism was ill-equipped to respond to the problems of the day, either in shaping personal character or having social relevance. Second, the Christians met the challenge of society with a message, through word and deed, that resulted in the final collapse of paganism and the rise of a Christian way of narrating the world.

The failure of paganism. How is it that pagans were unable to hold their own in the face of the epidemics, plagues and wars that resulted in the collapse of Rome? This question is very complicated, and I don't pretend to answer it in this book. However, noted social historians have observed trends that led to the collapse of pagan influence in the Roman Empire. These trends, part of the cycle of decay, are evident today in our Western culture. But more about that later.

First, religious pluralism, an essential feature of paganism, was unable to address the despair that resulted from the calamities of history. It has been said that those who believe in everything end up believing in nothing. Spiritual relativism was the one absolute in Roman society. No philosophy, cult or mystery religion claimed to have all truth. Religion in the Roman Empire rarely dealt with issues of truth. Religious practices were primarily cultic acts, rituals and festivals. The gods of paganism were to be feared and placated, not loved and served. In times of great crisis, when the physical world is harsh and cruel, the inner person cries out for something more than religious mechanisms designed to please an arbitrary god. Paganism simply had nothing to offer those whose personal lives, families and entire social network had been devastated by the travesties of the historical moment.

Second, the pagan attitude toward women—half of society—was so negative that it tore at the fabric of society. Women were treated as objects. Men who lived with no sexual regulation before or during marriage expected a different standard for women. Women were to be chaste until marriage and then faithful afterward. But men were sexually licentious. Furthermore, unwanted female infants were either drowned by their fathers or abandoned to die, unwanted simply because of gender. Abortion was rampant. Women were married off at age twelve or thirteen, often in unhappy arrangements made by their father. Widows who remarried were required to hand over their inheritance to the new husband, who by law became the owner of her and her possessions. Women were simply oppressed and subjugated to men.

Third, homosexuality was not only accepted but encouraged. Homosexual relations between men and boys were lauded and promoted by poets and philosophers. Homosexuals regarded themselves as an elite society of human beings, above the pedestrian and bland conjugal relations of a man with a woman. The combined effect of female infanticide and the celebration of the homosexual lifestyle led to a diminishment of the birth rate among pagans. As pagan families decreased in population, their influence in society also waned.

Fourth, the empire's failure to successfully handle epidemics and disasters, especially in the cities, led to a failure of confidence in the pagan way of life. The cities, small in space, were densely populated. Most people lived in apartment buildings—one family per room. Sanitation was practically nonexistent, with urine and feces often dumped from windows into streets no wider than a common path. The great bulk of people lived in squalor, dirt and filth, and among roaches, spiders, and infection-bearing insects. When a plague hit the cities, a third to a half of its occupants died. The stench from the dead bodies was unbearable. The pagans, interested primarily in their own welfare, fled the cities and abandoned their own families for the sake of survival.

For these reasons and more, pagan character was doomed to failure. As respect for pagans fell, so the confidence in the pagan message and way of life was lost. Many pagans, now in doubt about a way of life once affirmed, turned to the Christian message and way of life, which offered hope.

The Christian alternative. The Christian narration of the world stood in bold contrast to the pagan narration.

First, in contrast to religious pluralism, Christians were the people of one way. Pagan religion is based on the assumption that human beings must reach out to find and to placate God. The Christian narrative is that God initiates a relationship with humans. The one true God of God, Jesus Christ, actually becomes incarnate in our history, lives among us, takes up our suffering into himself, dies to destroy death and is raised to inaugurate the new creation. By faith and trust in him and baptism into his name, we are lifted into communion with the living God and subsequently live in the hope of a new heaven and earth. This radical message of God's love for humanity led pagans to abandon religious pluralism, which never touched their souls, and to turn to the life-changing, transformative good news offered in the name of Jesus.

This good news revolutionized the place of women in society. It was good news for all—men, women, children, the unborn—all peoples of all tribes and nations and colors and positions in life. It affirmed that all people are created in the image of God and must be treated with respect in the home, family and society.

> THE CHRISTIAN NARRATION OF THE WORLD STOOD IN BOLD CONTRAST TO THE PAGAN NARRATION.

Christians protected the sanctity of life, affirming the unborn child. Christians rescued abandoned female infants, taking them into their homes, where they were loved and made part of the family. Christian females married at a later age than pagans, had more choices and enjoyed more security in a marriage. Their husbands, following Christian teaching, remained faithful. Christian widows kept the estate of their husband, and widowhood was held in high regard within the church.

Christian sexual convictions were also a stabilizing element of society. The church taught against promiscuous behavior, homosexual relationships and infidelity. In contrast to pagan families, Christian families were more secure, produced more children and contributed to the general welfare of society.

The response of Christians to epidemics and other calamities were also in stark contrast to the pagans. The pagans had no message to give to the suffering masses. They had no narrative that would bring peace in the midst of crisis. They had no way to address the despair, hopelessness and meaninglessness of life felt by so many in the face of disaster. The Christians, on the other hand, offered a message of meaning and hope. God's involvement in history and his overcoming of the powers of evil and destruction gave hope in the midst of human pain and suffering. God himself, in a war against all that destroys life, had participated in death, defeated it and would ultimately triumph over all that is sin and death through the creation of a new heavens and earth. The Christian message provided hope in the midst of calamity.

Christians not only had a message, they exhibited a way of life that put flesh on the bones of that message. Christians remained in the cities, offered water, food and medical assistance to the dying, often lying next to and dying with them.

In brief, Christian character narrated the world differently. Both the pagans who were dying and those who lived could not help but observe the character of Christian conduct in matters of work, family, sexuality and the care of the sick and dying. Watching the lives of people who had been transformed by the message of God's creation, incarnation and re-creation turned many pagans to the faith that eventually shaped the very foundations of Western civilization. The admonition of Peter, "Live such good lives among the pagans that, though they accuse you of doing wrong, they may see your good deeds and glorify God" (1 Peter 2:12), was being fulfilled before their very eyes.

How the Christian Narrative Formed Western Civilization

In A.D. 410 the Visigoths invaded Rome. In the next two hundred years these and other barbaric people literally destroyed Roman civilization. Cities were turned to rubble, the elaborate political organization of Roman governance was dismantled, commerce came to a halt. The great roads that connected the cities were ruined, aqueducts weren't maintained and some were made useless. The once great and proud Roman society had collapsed and its families were scattered—living in the ruins and eking out an existence from the land.

During these two hundred years of chaos, the church and Christians everywhere stepped into positions of leadership—not positions of political power (which came later) but as servants of a society in despair. By A.D. 600 there was nothing left of Roman power, society and culture. But the church, its bishops, priests and deacons, was everywhere. The church—and only the church—was poised to give leadership to the Western world. From A.D. 600 to 800 the church emerged as the leader of the Western world, culminating in the crowning of Charlemagne as the emperor of the Holy Roman Empire on December 25, 800.

Augustine: **The City of God.** In order to understand what happened during that four hundred years, we must turn to Augustine, one of the most formidable early thinkers of the Western world. Augustine was born in A.D. 354 and died in 430. He lived during the critical years when Rome was invaded by the barbarians. Augustine's deep thought about the crumbling of Rome and the church's relationship to earthly political bodies led him to write his classic work *The City of God.* The twenty-two books that make up *The City of God* were written over a thirteen-year period (413-426).

In books 11-22, Augustine sets forth his philosophy of history. In sum, this complicated and thorough work reveals the stories of two "cities": (1) of those who follow God, and (2) or those who live in rebellion against the purposes of God in history.

The stories originate in the Garden and in the subsequent foundations of civilization between the Fall of humans into sin and Noah. The two cities are already seen in Cain and Abel. Cain serves self; Abel serves God. History unfolds these two cities: the city of God and the city of man.

The city of God is grounded in the history of Noah, Abraham, Moses, the children of Israel, the kingdom of David, the prophets and the church. In all this history, types are found of Jesus Christ and the church.

In Jesus Christ, the story of the world is fulfilled. The church is, on the other hand, a witness to God's city, where his intent for humanity will be ultimately fulfilled. However, the church is not perfect. Augustine argues that it is not so pure that it does not have within it those who rebel against God's purposes for humanity and the world. The wheat and the tares grow together. But the church, as God's witness to the eternal city, will endure to the end.

The history of the city of man is the history of those who seek to build civilization on self, indifferent toward God's purposes for the world. These civilizations, like the Greeks and the Romans, rise and fall. They do not endure. But, like the *earthly church* that has within it those who are not of God, the *city of man* also has within it those who serve God's purposes in the world.

The relationship between the two cities. This brief summary of the two cities points to an enduring problem that is with us even now: A philosophy of history that acknowledges two cities, one in the service of God (the church) and the other in the service of humanity (the state), raises the question, What is the relationship between the two? There are a variety of answers to this question, which we cannot pursue in depth. In broad terms, there are three Christian visions of the relationship between the church and the state:

1. The *separatists* argue for a countercultural understanding of the church. The two kingdoms are in utter antithesis. Christians are to live in one kingdom, the kingdom of God, but not the other, the kingdom of man. Some, like the Amish, cluster in their own culture, others like Mennonite and Brethren, refrain from political office and are vocal pacifists. They also pray for their enemies and seek to win them over through acts of love.

2. The *identifiers* argue that we live in both kingdoms simultaneously. Luther argued for life in the church under the spirit, and life in the state under the sword. As Christians we live in the constant tension between our service under God and the expectations of our service

under the state or in the world. Christians can serve in politics and even in the army in times of war. Christians live in two worlds simultaneously.

3. The *transformers* argue that the goal of the kingdom of God is to convert the kingdom of this world and bring it under the rule of God. Medieval Christendom brought the two cities together under the pope, who ruled both church and state under God. John Calvin, a passionate Reformer, argued for a transformational view of society that brought church and state together under the Word of God, not under the pope.

If we were to explore these three basic views (of course, there are other permutations of them), we would note that both the identifiers and the transformers argue that the Christian story should influence if not change the foundations of civilization and make a difference in ethics, arts, business, government and all other areas of life.

The Impact of God's Narrative on Western Culture

The Christian narrative that God has become involved in human history—incarnate, dead, buried risen and coming again—resulted in convictions that, until recently, dominated Western society. God's incarnate narrative in flesh means that the immaterial, invisible realities of the spiritual world can be communicated in this visible, tangible world.

This principle influenced the understanding of the place of the church in the world, gave rise to the arts, resulted in an ordered understanding of the world, formed the conviction of the basic rationality and comprehensibility of the world, and gave rise to Christian ethics and social responsibility.

First, God's narrative influenced the self-understanding of the church and its ministries. The church is seen as the continuation of the presence of God in the world, a living witness to God's narrative. Worship continually proclaims and enacts God's story. The sacraments communicate the saving effect of God's story. Unfortunately, medieval Catholicism moved away from the original purpose of the church as the people of God when it modeled the church after Israel and created a theocracy under the pope. Catholics then brought worship and the sacraments under the divine authority of the pope and turned them into institutional, governmental and even materialistic or market-driven conduits of grace. This misplacement of the faith ultimately necessitated the Reformation.

Second, the conviction of God's incarnate narrative in the world resulted in the explosion of the arts. God is no distant deity out of touch with the earthly sphere of life, but one who is made known in the beauty of nature and expressed in music and the arts. This conviction gave rise to the great music of the Western world—Gregorian chant, plainsong, polyphonic hymns, choral and instrumental music, the work of Johann Sebastian Bach and the great hymnody of the Protestant church (e.g., that of Charles Wesley). It also birthed Christian arts: icons, illuminated Bibles, stained glass and church architecture. Literature was also affected by God's narrative, producing great works like John Bunyan's *Pilgrim's Progress*, John Milton's *Paradise Lost* and the works of Fyodor Dostoyevsky, especially *Crime and Punishment*.

> GOD IS NO DISTANT DEITY OUT OF TOUCH WITH THE EARTHLY SPHERE OF LIFE.

Next, the narrative of God as Creator of the universe resulted in an ordered understanding of the world, which affected city planning, exploration and observation, the birth of science, and the origins of medicine. All the cities and villages of the Western world during the medieval era and into the first centuries of the modern era were built with the church at the center. Exploration and observation led to advances in mathematics, the mapping of the world, the scientific exploration of the order of nature, the investigation of the cosmos and the study of the human body in search of medical procedures and the healing arts.

Fourth, God's narrative furthermore birthed a sense of the rationality and comprehensibility of the created order, giving rise to Christian education. Christian education flourished in the monasteries through the *scriptorium*, where Scripture was meticulously copied and produced. Gradually monasteries became centers of learning, of commentary on Scripture and ultimately of theological training. Christian learning began to rise around cathedrals in the cities. At first these centers of study were informal, but by the thirteenth century more formal universities with set curricula emerged in places like Oxford, Paris and Rome. Thomas Aquinas, the greatest of all medieval philosopher-theologians, organized the Christian faith in his most celebrated work, *Summa Theologica* (1266-1273). Here, Thomas synthesized the Christian faith with Aristotelian philosophy.

Finally, because God's narrative in this world is a way of life, Christianity shaped the ethics of the Western world. Ethics, like many other matters that Christianity shaped, were long under discussion by the philosophers. But now the mandates for living were grounded in God's revelation in the law, in God's incarnate life in Jesus Christ and in apostolic teaching, especially that of Paul. The ethical principles of Christianity shaped matters of justice, economics, common morality and decency, sexuality, marriage, family and all human relations. These principles had a profound effect on society, not only in determining what is good but also marking out that which is bad and in need of punishment, such as thievery, murder and unjust or dishonest dealings between people.

Ancient Christianity was not the privatized faith it has become today. Today the influence of secularization has pushed the Christian narrative away from public matters. Christian faith, having become private and narcissistic, has very little influence in the university, the marketplace, law, politics and even ethics. It no longer plays a significant role in the foundational matters of Western civilization.

Narrating the World

Because I grew up in a very conservative Protestant home, I inherited a bad attitude toward the medieval period. But since I have studied the medieval era and have associated with many devout Catholics, I am now free from that attitude. Nevertheless, I am always taken aback by those who continue to be negative about today's Catholicism. I especially hear it when I talk to people about making changes in worship. I am always surprised and disheartened when I get the response, "But isn't that Catholic?"

Of course we don't want to return to the medieval era with a pope over both state and church, nor do we want to return to a time when salvation was perceived as attainable through works. But we must admit that the accomplishments of the twelfth century in particular—the great universities, cathedrals, works of art and literature, philosophy and even town planning—were immense.

> ALL CREATION IS
> RENDERED HOLY
> BY THE
> INCARNATION.

Within God's narrative the doctrine that has had the greatest influence on civilization is the incarnation. If God unites with his creation in order to re-create it himself, then there can be no distinction between the secular and the sacred. All creation is rendered holy by the incarnation. All creation is lifted through the humanity of Jesus to union with the divine. The center from which this doctrine should radiate in all the cities, towns and villages is the worship of the church. The church building, the liturgy itself, with all of its attending signs and symbols and especially the words of the Eucharistic prayer, clearly portray who gets to narrate the world.

In the meantime Muslims are narrating the world according to Allah. And to be fair, the late Muslim empire is impressive. Bernard Lewis, in his acclaimed work *What Went Wrong? The Clash Between Islam and Modernity in the Middle East*, points to Islamic civilization at its peak:

> Islam represented the greatest military power on earth. . . . It was the foremost economic power in the world . . . [with] a far-flung network of commerce and communications in Asia, Europe, and

Africa; . . . exchanging a variety of foodstuffs, materials and manufactures with the civilized countries of Asia. . . . To this rich inheritance scholars and scientists in the Islamic world added an immensely important contribution through their own observations, experiments, and ideas. In most of the arts and sciences of civilization, medieval Europe was a pupil and in a sense a dependent of the Islamic world.[2]

However, the world has changed since the medieval era: the Muslim defeat and sack of Constantinople in 1453, the Renaissance, then the Reformation and the Enlightenment—all changed the course of history. Since then, the Islamic world went into decline and is presently wracked by wars between its factions, and America emerged as a secular superpower. Now the Radical Islamic element, clinging to the memories of former greatness, seeks to bring down its main rival, the great Satan, Western civilization.

In the meantime, the Western church has lost its divine narrative, turning toward a Christianity of cultural accommodation.

Conclusion

In this chapter I have attempted to show the impact of God's narrative on the structures of society and life. I have illustrated the failure of paganism to address the despair of the Roman world: religious relativism that offered no hope, promiscuous sexuality, negative attitudes toward women and children, and the invasions of barbarian tribes.

I have shown how the Christian narrative provided a stable religious alternative to paganism in a time of great upheaval. It elevated women, provided a stable sexual ethic, established the centrality of the family and home in society, and served humanity in a time of sweeping epidemics, calamities and war.

Three centuries of faithfulness to God's narrative set the stage for the church's role in society during the medieval period. While many Christians see the downside of Christendom during this period, especially the control of the church over society, we must not forget the enormous contribution of the Christian narrative to the church's worship and spirituality, to the spread of the arts, to the ordered understanding of the world, to the convictions of rationality, and to the influence of Christian ethics on society in general. However, in the last five hundred years the impact of God's narrative in all these areas has gradually eroded.

One of the major problems the church faces today is that the Christian faith has been reduced from its public engagement of civilization to a private relationship with God. I don't want to take that personal relationship away from anybody—much less myself. I believe in and have experienced an intimate, personal relationship with God, especially through his active presence in the Word, bread and wine, the water of baptism, prayer and song and in contemplative silence.

However, as I have been arguing in this book, there is more to Christianity than the personal side of the faith—there is the cosmic side, the claim of Jesus Christ to be Lord of the universe—Creator, Redeemer and Ruler of all. What I am asking of us all is to think through what it means to proclaim "Jesus is Lord," especially in the current spiritual contest with both Radical Islam and narcissistic America.

Radical Islam makes a claim to world domination. Allah, it says, wills the entire world to be under his dominion. Radical Islam, following Muhammad and Shari'a law, has worked out what it looks like to live under Allah. Their message is complete submission to Allah in religious, political and economic ways. They have rules for family life, women, children, relationships, dress, personal hygiene and literally every aspect of life. In Islam there is no freedom, no personal choice or will. Everyone in all situations must submit to the will of Allah, who does not seem to be characterized by love, mercy or redemption.

American narcissism also makes a claim to domination—domination of our spiritual world. I am the center of *my* own universe. I am the creator and sustainer of my own private reality; everything revolves around my happiness, my well-being, my personal satisfaction. Even Christians reduce Jesus and the Christian faith to a means of securing our own happiness, instead of rightly recognizing and living our lives in joyful obedience to the One who made us in *his* image and sustains us for *his* purposes in the world.

If the Father of our Lord Jesus Christ is indeed involved in the re-creation of the world, in winning it back from the evil one, then Christians must go back to the Garden of Eden and reclaim God's original purposes for creatures and creation. We are the image-bearers of God, and we have been given the task of making this world the theater of God's glory. It is not only the inner chamber of the heart that should glow with the presence of God, but our culture too—our cities, our civilization, the whole of life.

Today, the Christian faith has lost its cosmic narrative. So Christians must recover this cosmic dimension of the faith, especially in the face of the threat of the whole world being under *either* Islamic law *or* the spell of narcissistic American consumerism.

Summary

- Paganism, then and now, will always fail to successfully narrate the world, for it does not have a solid foundation upon which to build a civilization.

- It is not biblical to think of the Christian faith exclusively in terms of an individual's relationship with God.

- The ancient understanding of the cosmic narrative of God influenced the foundation of Western civilization, producing great universities, works of art and literature, town planning, political and economic theories, laws of peace and justice, and freedom to live righteously.

- Radical Islam and the Muslim community in general pose a particular challenge to privatized Christianity. Their vision of the world is comprehensive, with all personal and public life in submission to the rule of Allah. Privatized Christianity fails to see God's cosmic narrative for world history.

- Today, we Christians need to learn from the early Christians' impact
  on Western civilization. We need to envision the glory of God ruling
  over every aspect of life.

Recommended Reading

Hill, Jonathan. *What Has Christianity Ever Done For Us? How It Shaped the Modern World.* Downers Grove, Ill.: InterVarsity Press, 2005.

Stark, Rodney. *The Rise of Christianity: How the Obscure, Marginal Jesus Movement Became the Dominant Religious Force in the Western World in a Few Centuries.* San Francisco: HarperSanFrancisco, 1997.

Notes

[1]Bernard Lewis, *What Went Wrong? The Clash Between Islam and Modernity in the Middle East* (New York: Perennial, 2002), pp. 6-7.

4

How the West Lost God's Narrative

Many people will recognize the name Francis Schaeffer, the guru of Christianity and culture in the 1960s and 1970s. Schaeffer was associated with Covenant Seminary in St. Louis in the 1960s, coming there from L'Abri in Switzerland to give lectures on a fairly regular basis—almost yearly. I entered the Th.M. program at Covenant in 1959 and taught at Covenant College and then Covenant Seminary from 1960 to 1968. During these years I heard Schaeffer speak about the secularization of the West and was influenced by his analysis.

It was through Schaeffer's emphasis on secularization that I became especially interested in the study of intellectual history, especially modern thinkers who moved us from the medieval world through the Reformation and into the modern era. This was the door that led me to paradigm thinking.

A historical paradigm can be described as a particular cluster of ideas dominant within a period of history that has a beginning and ending. Where the paradigm begins and ends is somewhat arbitrary but generally observable. However, within the paradigm are the social, cultural, political, economic, religious and intellectual ideas that give shape to a *particular way of thinking*.

I became especially fond of paradigm thinking because my studies to date had focused on understanding theology within historical context. What kind of influence did the social and intellectual ideas of the day have on theological thinking and writing? Ideas have consequences, and these consequences filter into every area of life.

In the Western world we can observe six paradigms—biblical, ancient, medieval, Reformation, modern and the emerging postmodern. This chapter deals with the modern paradigm and the particular combination of ideas that gave rise to the process of secularization. I define *secularization* as "the movement away from historical religious sensibilities to a new condition of life." This chapter deals with "the movement away." It asks, How did we move from the ancient, medieval and Reformation ways of narrating the world—through the God of the Bible—to the present indifference to God and denial of his cosmic narrative? What I primarily hope to demonstrate is that reason and science in the modern world, which originally developed among Christians, eventually became the enemy of God's narrative by separating the secular from the sacred and thereby opening the possibility for new gods to narrate the world.

When I say that the West has lost God's narrative, I do not mean to suggest that the outline of God's narrative has been lost. What has been lost is, first, the full *interpretation* of the story that lies behind the narrative framework, and second, the *impact* of this narrative on the formation of society.

How did this change occur? How is it that the story of God, which once shaped the church and influenced the foundation of civilization, was lost?

Broadly speaking, there are two trends that resulted in the demise of God's narrative in the Western world: the secularization of Western culture, and the reduction of the faith through cultural accommodation. Before looking at these trends, we must find the cause that lies behind the secularization of the world and the reshaping of faith.

Why Did the West Fall Prey to Secularism?

Why did the West, which was once so thoroughly influenced by the

Christian faith, fall prey to secularism and privatism? The answer to that question is a very complex historical and theological issue. The key factor is the historical split between the secular and the sacred. This split occurred because the understanding of the incarnation was reduced from God who *became* the created order to God who *stepped into* the creation. Let me explain.

The historic understanding of the incarnation. What lies at the heart of the Christian faith is the conviction that God is both Creator and Redeemer. He redeems what he creates. "For God was pleased to have all his fullness dwell in him, and through him to reconcile to himself all things . . . by making peace through his blood, shed on the cross" (Col 1:19-20).

What God creates is good. The Fall is not an imprisonment in matter but a spiritual rebellion. Humanity chooses to direct life and unfold culture not according to the mandate of God but under the direction of the dark powers and principalities of this world. This, of course, affects life in the world. Instead of doing God's will in creation and making this world a theater of God's glory, humanity does the will of the evil one and turns life toward violence, hate, greed and the like. Humanity, which God created, then manifests evil in every structure of life— political, economic, institutional, ideological, family and personal relationships. So the world of God's creation, as Paul writes, is "subjected to frustration" and in "bondage to decay" (Rom 8:20, 21).

> AT THE HEART OF THE CHRISTIAN FAITH IS THE CONVICTION THAT GOD IS BOTH CREATOR AND REDEEMER.

The biblical and historical understanding of the incarnation is that God *becomes* creation. He takes into himself all the effects of fallen humanity spread throughout his creation. He assumes all of creation in the womb of Mary in order to reverse the effects of sin and "bring it into the glorious freedom of the children of God" (Rom 8:21). The death and resurrection of God in Christ is then not a "release of the soul from its imprisonment to the material realm" (as Gnostics and the new spirituality assert) but a second act of creation, the redemption of the whole created order. Now, as Paul states, "the whole creation [is] groaning as in the pains of childbirth right up to the present time" (Rom 8:22). That is, the whole creation has been "born again" so to speak, and now waits for its final deliverance. The whole creation, from the perspective of the Christian narrative, is pregnant and awaiting redemption.

The ancient church fathers developed a saying to capture the cosmic nature of the incarnation and subsequent redemption. The saying made popular in the ancient church is, "only that which is assumed can be redeemed." In other words, God, in the incarnation, took up into himself the entire creation, so that the creation redeemed by God himself is now to be once again, as in the Garden, the theater of his glory.

The ancient church understood the impact of creation, incarnation and re-creation on all of creation, and that is why Christians were the leaders in the arts, in learning and in the sciences. The Christian faith narrates the world and gives shape to culture-making and to all of civilization.

The modern approach to the incarnation. The historic understanding of the incarnation as the assumption of the entire created order has been replaced by a view that in the incarnation God *stepped into* history to save souls. The focus is no longer on the cosmic work of God in history but on personal salvation. The language often used to describe salvation through Christ expresses this shift. We speak of God "saving souls." We focus then not so much on God who redeems the world but on Christ who saved *me*.

Obviously it is true that God has saved *me*. We don't want to lose that personal touch. What I decry here is the loss of the cosmic vision, the idea that God's work of redemption narrates the entire world. The history of the world from beginning to end and all that it entails—its political, economic, artistic, psychological and scientific establishments—the whole of God's creation and all of life, has been redeemed because God in the incarnation received it all to himself. God redeemed all of life by the cross and empty tomb, so that when he returns to the earth not just souls but all of creation will be made perfect. In his first coming he defeated sin and death. In his second coming he will put away forever sin and death and all its consequences, and restore his Garden in the new heavens and earth and rule over all creation.

The assumption that the true me is a soul that lives inside of and is redeemed from the body to soar into some kind of ethereal realm is not Christian, it is gnostic. And this is the primary spirituality of the New Age religion of our time (more on this in chap. 5). The current misunderstanding of the incarnation logically results in a split between the sacred and the secular because if Christ only redeems souls, the stuff of this world is unredeemable. This split in turn resulted in our loss of God's narrative of the world. Modernity began to see creation and all of life apart from God. The origin, meaning and destiny of the world found new gods in reason and science. Creation separated from redemption will always result in the secularization of life.

The Secularization of the West

The Renaissance versus the Reformation. We find the split between the secular and the sacred emerging in the Renaissance and the Reformation. The Renaissance marked the transition from the medieval to the modern era. Gradually expanding from the fourteenth through the sixteenth centuries, it spread over Western Europe and contributed greatly to the end of the influence of the church in the world. It secularized life, infusing into philosophy, religion, politics and art a new spirit of human freedom. No longer subjected to ecclesiastical jurisdiction and dogmatic creedalism, humanity was elevated to the center of the universe. Renaissance scholars and artists exalted the power of reason and sought to interpret and understand the world apart from the strictures of traditional thought. Here the significance and the importance of Renaissance humanism as a break from God is found. It was an attempt, unaided by anything outside of self, to interpret and control the world—a spirit of total self-sufficiency. This spirit called for and ultimately generated a secularized culture.

On the other hand, the Reformation influenced the Western world toward the sacred. Although the Reformation was mainly a doctrinal renewal—a rediscovery of biblical Christianity over against the misinterpretation imposed by Roman dogma and tradition—it nevertheless also influenced the world of politics, philosophy, science and art.

The Reformers viewed life as a unified reality. This incarnational view saw life as a whole, believing that all endeavors within life were religious in nature. That is, people either directed all of their activities toward God or toward self. This gave rise to a reinterpretation of vocation which taught that, for the Christian, *all* work was religious activity. The world was conceived as God's world, which set the Christian free to do art, politics, philosophy, economics and science as an act of worship. There is no divorce between the secular and the sacred. Work, pleasure, family and worship are all related to the service of God.

The significance of the Reformation therefore lies in the Reformers' conviction that God narrates the whole world. The movement called for a religion of the whole person involved in all of culture. It called for a world under God, a society shaped by Christian principles, a people informed by a biblical worldview, serving and enjoying God in all of life. The genius of the Reformation lay in the freedom to see the individual under God, to understand the world as the arena of religious activity, and to place God at the center of life, giving meaning to history and culture.

Thus, in the sixteenth century these two cultures—Renaissance and Reformation—posed two alternative narratives of the world. One was human-centered; the other was God-centered. Sadly, the Reformation narrative has been lost. The human-centered narrative has become dominant in the West. Even the church allows itself to be shaped by ideas that grew out of the secularization of the West.

The secularizing influence of the Renaissance on modernity. Renaissance culture gradually gave rise to humanism and rationalism, the breeding ground for widespread secularism. Tracing these movements through history allows us to understand the depth of the secularization of the West and the reasons why the Christian narrative has been swallowed up by secularism.

The humanistic narrative is neither medieval nor "enlightened." Humanism stands somewhere between, born of a reaction against medieval habits of mind, ideals, cosmology and religion, but without the rational understanding of new habits that were to be developed in the Enlightenment age. Humanists, as scholars of the Greek and Roman culture, expressed their yen for learning through art: architecture, sculpture and painting. Humanists were rebels who found the medieval way of life unlovely, untrue and dull. They wanted to open the windows to let some fresh air in.

Humanism gave birth to an era of rationalism. The basic difference between humanists and rationalists can be understood by comparing artists and scientists. While humanists are dreamers, rationalists to some extent fulfill their dreams. The humanistic emphasis on nature led the rationalists to investigate nature. Through their emphasis on the details of nature, humanist artists conceived of the universe as machine-like; the rationalists discovered the laws which demonstrated that the world ran like a machine. The humanistic political theory of Machiavelli, which conceived of the state as an end in itself, was put into practice by the rationalists in the French Revolution. In his *Utopia*, Thomas More dreamed of a world in which humans, living according to their good nature, would work virtuously with their fellow humans; the rationalists attempted to fulfill this dream through the doctrine of progress, which looked forward to an ultimate utopia based on the view that the world was rapidly becoming better.

> THE HUMAN-CENTERED NARRATIVE HAS BECOME DOMINANT IN THE WEST.

Two significant discoveries eventually separated science and knowledge from the divine narrative and contributed to the secularization of the West. The first discovery is the area of cosmology. Nicolaus Copernicus (1473-1543) discovered that the earth swings around the sun once in a year, and at the same time the earth turns on its own axis once a day. The spread of Copernicus's discovery was assured by the appearance of two "new" stars in the heavens. Through astronomical observations Johannes Kepler (1571-1630) was able to determine certain laws by which he was able to chart the movement of planets. Thus, based on the assertion of a mechanical universe that ran on its own, the stage was set for those who would divorce science from God's narrative.

The second discovery was in the area of epistemology, which attempts to answer the question, How do we know? Medieval epistemology looked to the authority of the church, while the Reformers looked to the Scriptures. In either case, the authority came from beyond the world. But authority shifted to autonomous reason, observation and scientific testing.

A new way of knowing. Enlightenment epistemology shifted from religious authority to human reasoning through three influential men. First, Francis Bacon (1561-1626) contributed greatly to the rise of the scientific attitude. In his book *New Atlantis* he proposed a society based on science. The community was to contain a house of science and technique, a laboratory, a bureau of planning and a workshop. Second, René Descartes (1596-1650) located knowledge not in external authority but in human reason: "I think, therefore I am." Third, John Locke (1632-1704) located authority in human experience. Having overthrown the concept of innate ideas, Locke suggested that humans are shaped entirely by their environment. This view was to have its full effect later when people became convinced that the manipulation of the environment would eliminate most problems and produce good humans and a peaceful, utopian society. The view that knowledge derives from reason, experience and the scientific method naturally contributed to the breakdown of a supernatural concept of life and gave rise to the naturalistic worldview.

These three ideas, which took hold in the eighteenth-century, suggested the possibility of quickly achieving an earthly utopia through human reason and effort. However, new adjustments to this world narrative resulted from subsequent developments made during the nineteenth century. These came first through the work of biologists, especially Charles Darwin. Geological research also indicated that life had been on earth for many thousands of years. Fossil remains suggested that life moved from the simple to the complex, that life was progressing in an ascending scale. Consequently, humans came to be viewed as the final triumph of living organisms. The idea of evolution seemed to argue against achieving utopia quickly; the change from the old environment was now viewed as a transition instead of a leap.

Another modification was brought about through the rise of nationalism. The evolutionary idea of the struggle of the fittest was incorporated into the struggle between organized groups, classes of people and nation-states—the roots of communism.

By the beginning of the twentieth century it was quite clear that a new narrative (or narratives) had emerged. The biblical story of God had emerged out of the ancient period of history and had influenced the foundations of the Western world, but now both the medieval and Reformation narratives were replaced by a secular narrative. Humanity—its origins, meaning and destiny—no longer needed the divine narrative. Reason, science, evolution, progress—these ideas replaced the old narrative of creation, incarnation and re-creation. The world could be understood without God.

Twentieth-century secularism. The twentieth century opened on the romantic notion of a utopia based on the progress of humanity through science, reason and an evolutionary principle at work in the universe through which the ideal would be achieved. However, the optimism of the early decades quickly gave way to pessimism about the future of humanity. World War I, "the war to end all wars," was rapidly followed by the Great Depression and World War II. The atrocities of World War II challenged the whole structure of utopianism. The idea of progress was shattered; the concept of the goodness of humanity could not stand in the face of the facts. Industry and science, which were to have served the needs of humanity, were now turned against humanity and used as instruments of destruction. *Despair* rather than *hope* became the byword.

After the war, conditions did not improve. A new kind of person emerged. Rather than being characterized by the free, autonomous spirit of utopia, the human scene was dominated by the impersonal mass, by conformity to the suburban ideal. Humanity was not free; people were trapped like animals in an unhealthy environment, threatened by poisonous air and water as well as by overpopulation. Psychological stress became dominant as the future of humanity's very existence began to be questioned.

Out of this present situation two attitudes emerged. The first, an attitude of despair, expresses itself in an absurdist philosophy of life. Absurdity, which is the logical conclusion of secularism, regards life as totally meaningless. Humans are biological animals produced by chance, with no purpose in life except death—the ultimate absurdity. A person's only alternative is to authenticate the self, to "do your thing," to do whatever you want in any given situation. Released from all religious, moral or social norms, each person becomes his or her own final reference point. "Do what you want to do" becomes the motto of life. Only the restraints of society keep the world from total chaos in this situation. The significance of this attitude is that the utopian hope is gone. The dream world has come crashing down.

> ABSURDITY, WHICH IS THE LOGICAL CONCLUSION OF SECULARISM, REGARDS LIFE AS TOTALLY MEANINGLESS.

The impact of secularism can also be seen in the rise of the new intellectualism. The new intellectual describes our present ills as a result of our inability to keep up with the development of science. While science has produced a new world, humans have not significantly changed. The hope of the world now lies in the control of humanity and the environment. Persons can and should be controlled through the behavioral sciences. New creatures can be produced through scientific advancement. Patterns of behavior can be introduced through new drives in the unconscious and new ideas of right and wrong in the superego. Thus, through scientific conditioning, humans can and should be made better. An elite few will decide what kind of a society and what kind of a human being is most desirable. Significantly, we have shifted away from the romantic ideal of progress and have adopted a utopian ideal based on manipulation and control.

The Western world of the twentieth-century was basically secular and humanistic. Secular humanism looks within the universe for its structure of meaning and authority for life. No matter what type of humanism—whether it be the exuberant humanism of the Renaissance, the rationalism of the Enlightenment, the Romanticism of the nineteenth century or the despair of modernity—it is incapable of offering hope because it does not view the world as God's creation. Because secularism does not deal with reality, it cannot succeed as a worldview. It is doomed to repeat the cycle of optimism followed by despair. Humanity cannot rule itself. Autonomous humanity's attempt to narrate the world without God has a long record of failure.

In a world that focuses on itself as ultimate and final, where secularism reigns and there is no longer a meaningful narration of the world, people inevitably begin to search elsewhere for answers and security. It is in the mayhem of this secular world that Radical Islam has emerged, offering a world narrator quite unknown in the West—Allah, who is understood as the true storyteller of the world and who guides life by Shari'a law.

Can the Christian faith in its present state, having been sorely weakened by secularization, withstand the Islamic narrative? Obviously we live with the promise that the gates of hell cannot overcome the church. I believe that! But we would be very foolish indeed if we did not recognize that Muslims have invaded Christian lands in the past, subdued them and brought vast areas of the world under Islamic law.

In the past Muslims have made two attempts at world domination. In a hundred-year period between the mid-seventh and mid-eighth century, Muslims conquered lands occupied by Christians. They integrated all states from the peninsula of Syria, Egypt and Iran into a unified state under the control of Medina, the central holy city. Then, in that same period, they attacked Byzantium and spread into North Africa and Spain. These lands, once populated by Christians, came under Muslim control. The second attempt at world domination occurred between the fifteenth and seventeenth centuries during the Ottoman bid for world control. Now, after nearly three hundred years of quiet, the Islamic fundamentalists have renewed their bid for world domination. Radical Islam and its many terrorist supporters throughout the world have positioned themselves against Israel, against Western culture and against Christians. This is no idle threat. Are Christians ready? Do Christians know the Christian narrative? Will Christians die for their faith?

The Reduction of Faith Through Cultural Accommodation

To complicate matters other insidious shifts have been taking place under the umbrella of secularization—the reduction of God's cosmic narrative among liberal Christians to a social program for the betterment of the world, and a reduction of God's cosmic narrative among evangelicals to a focus on the narrative of one's own experience of faith.

The cultural accommodation of modern liberals: Social betterment. The reduction of the faith to social betterment was a Christian response to the nineteenth-century industrial revolution. The industrial revolution was not to the advantage of all peoples. Only a few benefited from the increased production while many suffered, especially in the city where cheap labor gave rise to economic stratification: the extreme wealth of the rich and the ghetto conditions of the poor. Liberal Christians, under the leadership of Walter Rauschenbusch (1861-1918), developed a theological social ethic based on the dialectical understanding (thesis-antithesis-synthesis) of history set forth by Georg W. F. Hegel (1770-1831). Rauschenbusch pointed to the preaching of Jesus about the kingdom of righteousness. The kingdom, he argued, was the ultimate good world that Christ taught about, based on love, justice and righteousness. It is the goal of the church to achieve this utopian world. The church must contribute to the upward process of history. It must

progressively relieve the conditions of the poor, thereby establishing a society of righteousness and love where all humans would dwell together
in fellowship and peace. This view was fostered by the idea of the father-
hood of God and the infinite value of the human soul, a conviction that
gave rise to a socially conscious church dominant in the first half of the
twentieth century. This church was driven by a program of world reha-
bilitation. Unfortunately, among the liberal Christians God's supernatural narrative of creation, incarnation and re-creation was replaced by a
do-gooder church changing the world through social action.

Social action is an essential aspect of the church's work in the world—
peace and justice and caring for the poor, widows, orphans, the disenfran-
chised, and the marginalized arise from true faith. But these actions are
to result from the *embodiment* of God's full narrative, not from a Christianity accommodating itself to Western culture's doctrine of progress
and utopia.

The cultural accommodation of conservatives: privatism. The second shift, reducing the faith to personal experience, was the result of
nineteenth-century Romanticism's impact on revivalism. The Romantics
rejected rationalism and looked instead to intuition and personal experience as their authority.

Revivalism was influenced by the romantic notion of truth based on
experience. Revivalists of the nineteenth and twentieth centuries called
for personal conversion that had to be verified by reference to a dateable
experience. One had to say, in effect, "on May 3, 1913, at 9:30 in the evening, at a revival in First Church, I repented of my sin and turned to Jesus
as my Savior. I know I am saved because of that experience and the feeling
of forgiveness I received."

The problem to which I point is not the experience itself; many people
have had life-changing experiences at revivals, and for that we give thanks
to God. The problem is that people began to *focus* on the experience.
They testified to the experience, dwelled on the experience, created a
spirituality that reflected on the experience and repeatedly attempted to
recover its feeling.

Historic Christianity is not a reflection on an individual's narrative but a reflection on and contemplation of God's mighty deeds of salvation for the life of the world. God's narrative is to grasp the heart and transform the believer. However, revivalism focuses on the believer's experience. This shift to experience has led to the demise the narrative of God. God rescues the entire created order, and those who know this rescue are to live collectively in the world and express God's redemption in all of life. This narrative has been lost and replaced with a focus on "my journey." Because liberals and conservatives lost God's cosmic narrative, they have been unable to offer a viable challenge to the dominant secular narrative of the world.

Conclusion

When Christianity narrated the world, it did so out of the conviction that the divine and human were united in the incarnate Word, Jesus Christ. He is both Creator and Redeemer. The process of secularization wrenched the divine from the human. At first it stole the divine presence from history, then from the world, then from the church's worship and sacraments, and finally from Jesus himself (among the liberals), who was stripped of his divinity.

No longer narrated by divine presence and divine destiny, Christianity fell prey to humanistic social betterment (among liberals) and attention to experience (among evangelicals), with its accompanying privatism, pragmatism and consumerism. This kind of secularized Christianity will most likely fold under the pressures of Radical Islam. Let me unpack the reasons.

First, under the influence of secularism, the Christian faith has come to rely on reason or science or experience. I am not suggesting there is no place for these in the explanation or defense of the Christian faith. What I point to is the reliance and trust we place in our well-worked-out reasons, scientific proofs or life changing experience. We say, "Look, I really can demonstrate the message of the Bible to be true—consider the persuasive power of this logical fact or the undisputable argument of that scientific conclusion or the new life I live." But when we argue this way, we overlook the inner authority of the Scripture and seek to support it with an external authority. Truth is made dependent on something outside the authority of the Bible. We judge the Bible by bringing it under a discipline: reason, science, experience or some other field of study. We must do the opposite—bring all the disciplines *under* the Word of God, under God's narrative from beginning to end.

God's view of life, which is found in the Bible, is his total and comprehensive narrative. It does not need to be shored up by this or that discipline.

God's narrative stands on its own as the truth about the world. We don't ask God to conform to our narrative, to our reasons, scientific findings, philosophy or anthropology. No, God invites us to live in his narrative and to see all of life from inside the lens of creation, incarnation and re-creation.

The spiritual face-off with Radical Islam is not a battle of reason, science or philosophy. It is a clash of narratives.

What narrative do you live by?

Muslims have their story of a deterministic God to whom we all owe utter external obedience in order to please him. And for Radical Islam this includes religious coercion and conformity by the tip of the sword, if necessary.

Christians have their story of a loving Creator who, in the incarnation, lifts broken and alienated humanity into his incarnate Word and delivers humans from the curse of sin and death by Christ's cross and empty tomb. He will return to rescue the whole world and rule over his entire creation with peace and justice.

Back to paradigms. The Radical Islamic way is a completely different paradigm of thought than any of the Western paradigms. They

> BECAUSE LIBERALS AND CONSERVATIVES LOST GOD'S COSMIC NARRATIVE, THEY HAVE BEEN UNABLE TO OFFER A VIABLE CHALLENGE TO THE DOMINANT SECULAR NARRATIVE OF THE WORLD.

skipped the modern paradigm and were never affected by the attempt to prove their faith through reason and science. Therefore, to assume that they will reason with Western Christians and come to tolerate our paradigm and way of thinking is futile. It is story versus story. Holy Spirit versus *jihad*.

Standing up to be counted is not just standing for Jesus but for the whole story of God, of which Jesus is the centerpiece. But that is not easy in a post-Christian, postmodern, neopagan world.

Summary

- The emphasis on reason and science in the modern world, which originally developed among Christians, eventually became the enemy of God's narrative by making a distinction between the secular and sacred, opening the possibilities for new gods to narrate the world from completely secular perspectives. Now the radical Muslims unite the secular-sacred with their world-dominating message.

- The loss of God's narrative in the West does not mean that the outline of God's narrative has been lost. What has been lost is, first, the full interpretation of the story that lies behind the narrative framework, and, second, the impact of this narrative on the forming of society.

- In the incarnation God lifted up into himself the entire creation, so that the redeemed creation is once again, as in the Garden, the theater of his glory.

- By the beginning of the twentieth century it was quite clear that a new narrative (or narratives) had emerged. The story of God, which had emerged out of the ancient period of history and had influenced the foundations of the Western world, has now been replaced by a secular narrative. Humanity—its origins, meaning and destiny—no longer believes it needs the divine narrative. Reason, science, evolution and progress—these ideas replace the old narrative of creation, incarnation, re-creation. The world can now be understood without God.

Recommended Reading

Tarnas, Richard. *The Passion of the Western Mind: Understanding the Ideas That Have Shaped Our World View.* New York: Ballantine, 1991.

5

Our Postmodern, Post-Christian, Neopagan World

We now live in a world that has no unified narrative, a world much like the Roman Empire in which the Christian narrative first appeared. Obviously our world is not exactly the same as the Roman world. We are not under a Caesar. We live in a world of advanced industry and technology. What is similar is that, like the early Christians, we live in a world of moral decadence, of many philosophical options and of religious pluralism. This is the *setting* in which the most pressing spiritual issue of the day—who gets to narrate the world?—must be answered. This question cannot be adequately answered by a culturally conditioned faith.

I certainly am not the only one who feels this way. There is a growing cadre of Christian leaders and laypersons who feel that our current ministry practices are inadequate for the challenges of the postmodern, post-Christian, neopagan society. As society comes to a dead-end street, will Radical Islam step in to narrate the world, or will the world-encompassing narrative of Christianity become viable again?

This is a question our young leaders are asking. I first experienced discontent among the younger leaders back in the mid-1990s. I was doing workshops on worship throughout North America. In every city where I conducted workshops I met young people who expressed their concerns about the nature of our society and the church's ineffectiveness. For the most part they expressed their discontent and unwillingness to continue in the same direction the church had traveled since the mid-1970s. However, I discovered they had no real answer to the problem. They were bewildered about the future and what to do about our society and the church. I didn't realize it at the time, but I was talking to the young people who would soon organize around Brian McLaren's leadership in what has come to be known as the "emerging church."

We are up against what seems to be insurmountable problems in a society suffering the consequences of losing God's narrative of the world. In this chapter I address the issues that these younger leaders are seeing in our society.

We Live in a World of Moral Decadence

There was a time when the Christian narrative so thoroughly penetrated our culture that its moral teachings served as a restraint on society. Today, in a time when the Christian narrative has been lost, moral behavior has gone through an unprecedented unraveling and subsequent failure.

Because there is no god, secular humanism has argued that human beings must take their destiny into their own hands. It is necessary for humans to establish universal rules based on reason for the behavior of humanity—both personal and collective. These rules were to normalize human relations, curb violence and war, and result in worldwide peace.

However, the efforts of the humanists have failed, and we now live in a posthumanist era in which there are no universal rules. In the past fifty years there has been a gradual breakdown of the Christian understanding of what it means for humanity to be crowned with the dignity of being made in the image of God.

The most striking example of an antihuman morality is the 1973 *Roe v. Wade* decision on abortion. Abortion, it was argued, will solve the problem of unwanted children, especially children born into poverty. Instead, abortion has unleashed a culture of violence that has resulted not only in the degradation of the unborn child but also in a morality that regards the human being as less important than the planet and animals.

For some, animals have more rights than a human being. Recently, a squirrel appeared in my attic. I called the animal humane society to ask how to get rid of it. The first words out of the mouth of the person to whom I spoke were, "You know you can't kill it. It is against the law to kill an animal. You could incur a fine and even go to jail."

"Oh," I responded. "That's just great. We live in a society where you can kill an unborn child, but you can't harm a squirrel. What kind of a world is that?" In a society where human beings are on the same level (or below) with animals, morality ceases to have a point of reference.

Personal morality has undergone a revolution. While statistics are not available, I believe that personal moral behavior in the West is about where it was in Rome when Christianity first appeared. Premarital sex, adultery, pornography, homosexuality and even bestiality are quite common. The sexual revolution has deeply affected the family, is breaking down marriage and is undermining the stability of society. In education the homosexual lifestyle is presented as a positive option. The media—especially television, movies and popular magazines—laud and glorify sexual freedom and alternative lifestyles. Pornography is easily accessed through the Internet and has contributed greatly to the sexual abuse of children.

> WE NOW LIVE IN A POSTHUMANIST ERA IN WHICH THERE ARE NO UNIVERSAL RULES.

Christians live and move and have their being in this amoral cultural climate. The narrative of our world denies that humanity is made in the image of God. It also denies that the Creator reveals how we are to live. God's purpose in making us for himself and creating us to be in community with him and each other is ignored—in large part because it is simply not known. For these reasons, God's narrative for intentional, obedient and fulfilling respect for human life and sexual relations is a revolutionary message in our world of lost narrative.

We Live in a World of Philosophical Relativism

Today's philosophical relativism is certainly not exactly like that of the Roman era, primarily because there are new and different philosophical constructs. But like the philosophy of the ancient era, today's philosophical contenders make no claim to provide a universal narrative that explains the origin, meaning and destiny of life.

The ancient Greek world was not particularly philosophical. The Greeks explained the world through religious myths—especially myths of the Olympian deities such as Apollo, the god of light and music, or Athena, the goddess of wisdom and war. However, the Greeks began to break from religious myths through the influence of Socrates and Plato in the fifth century B.C., and Aristotle in the fourth century B.C. These new philosophers argued for a universal mind, the *logos*. The logos was a kind of intelligent design that provided the world with a rational structure. The human mind, they argued, is also rational, and thus capable of participating in the universal rationality of the world. For this reason it is possible for the human mind to understand the world.

This ancient concept of rationality was quite different from the rationality of the modern era. In the ancient world rationality was a property of the world to which the reasonable human mind conformed. However, in the modern world reason is reduced to human consciousness. The individual mind possesses the power of reason, which can be applied to the world, which is an object of human inquiry. Reason, it is argued, is not intrinsic to the world and to all of creation, as the ancients thought. Instead, human beings have the capacity to think and rationally determine values and ways for people to live in harmony with each other.

This form of subject-object reason is used to refute the existence of God. The three most prominent rationalists who formed the secular way of thinking about the world are Charles Darwin (1809-1882), Sigmund Freud (1856-1939) and Karl Marx (1818-1883). Darwinian evolution answered the question, Where did we come from? Marx answered the question, What is human destiny? with his ironclad understanding of history moving humanity toward a communal goal. And what is the meaning of life? Freud, rejecting God, insisted that human beings must find meaning within themselves.

However, secular humanism has been trumped by the arrival of postmodern philosophy. Postmodernism rejects all attempts to express a metanarrative—a single, authoritative narrative—of the world. Postmoderns argue against all philosophical certainty, whether that of Darwin, Marx or Freud. Postmoderns argue that we have come to the end of all theories and explanations of the world. If there is one absolute, it is that there is no universal, no complete interpretation of life. All attempts at a comprehensive vision of the world are foolish and useless. We must learn to live without a universal narrative that gives meaning to life. Thus, Jean-François Lyotard (1924-1998) defines postmodernism as the "incredulity of the meta-narrative."

The assumption that there are no moral standards, that knowledge cannot be attained and that all ethical and metaphysical thought is worthless and empty has led to the condition of nihilism. Nihilism is the conviction that there is no intrinsic meaning to life. The twentieth-century philosopher Martin Heidegger (1889-1976) attempted to understand humanity without God (or some other higher being) and concluded that humans must assert their own being. In the face of the absence of an eternal being as a point of reference, Heidegger argued that humans should simply face the arbitrary nature of the world's nothingness, make a decision to be, and live an intentional and authentic life, a life of their own *being*. In the end, living in a postmodern world gives us nothing to believe in but ourselves, and that can only end in despair.

We Live in a World of Religious Pluralism

In spite of the fact that we live in a world without a unified narrative, religion abounds. But the popular religions of the day are not religions with a narrative but the religions of escape. The New Age religions that have swept our secular world have turned us toward a secular, generic spirituality. They have reenchanted our world with the experience of transcendence—calling on us to find our meaning "outside of this world in a religious experience of 'otherness.' "

Secularism undermined the Christian narrative. The triune God, who created and became incarnate to re-create will at the end of history establish the new heavens and the new earth, is no longer known. Nonetheless, we live in a very religious world. Secularism opened the door for the restoration of all the ancient religions.

Walk into Borders or Barnes & Noble bookstore, grab a cup of coffee and stroll over to the religion section—one of the largest book sections in the store. There you will find a spate of books on ancient religions and religions of the East. You can read about the ancient Persian religion Zoroastrianism, the Greek god Zeus, Egyptian mystery cults, the Norse religions of the Vikings, goddess worship of the ancient Celts, Buddhism, Hinduism and Jainism. Explore the Asian religions of Confucianism, Shinto and Taoism. Read all you want about Islam or Native American religions.

In almost every religion the quest is to find a way to transcend the pain and suffering of life, and get connected with the powers of the other world that will help us endure this world. Current magazines, movies and spiritual gurus pitch the supernatural. But in these religions we never hear that God himself has entered our history and our suffering to redeem us for life in this world. Instead, the message is something like this: Follow these practices and you can get in touch with the other world. You will momentarily escape this world and find principles for living that will help you cope with the drudgery of life. You can gain a supernatural power that will help you find release from imprisonment in your material body. The counter-Christian faith of the new gnosticism is perhaps the most prominent of all these escape religions.

We Live in a World Where Christianity Is Being Redefined

In chapter two I wrote about the first- and second-century competitor to New Testament Christianity: Gnosticism. Gnosticism is back and very popular. Ancient Gnosticism combined elements from Christianity with Zoroastrianism and the Greek mystery cults to create a compelling mythological narrative of the world. Like most religions it is dualistic, positing an eternal conflict between the invisible, spiritual world, which is good, and the material world, which is evil. This dualism holds a special attraction today for people who feel trapped in the material world.

The concept of imprisonment is central to all gnostic teaching. The real you is an invisible spirit. It is trapped in a physical body in a material world. The real you has got to escape this material entrapment! That is salvation—an experience of the transcendent.

The new gnosticism originated with the discovery of the ancient Gnostic texts in Nag Hammadi, Egypt, in 1945. It took some time for these texts to become known, to be translated and to trickle into our contemporary consciousness. These Gnostic texts present a very different kind of Christianity than historic orthodox Christianity. They date back to the second through the fourth centuries A.D. and teach a dualism that fits well with the pattern of dualism we find today in the New Age philosophy and religion. Salvation is an experience of transcendence—a momentary experience of otherness that leads to peace and tranquility.

Gnosticism has been made popular by Dan Brown's *The Da Vinci Code* and is now advocated in a nonfiction book, *The Jesus Papers*, by Michael Baigent.

The message of Jesus according to the new gnostics. Baigent is already well known for his work *Holy Blood, Holy Grail*. In this book he and his colleagues first set forth the theory that Jesus Christ and Mary Magdalene married and established a historical bloodline. *The Da Vinci Code* expounds on this theory.

In *The Jesus Papers* Baigent wants the world to know that the orthodox Christianity that overcame the Gnostics of the early church and influenced the foundations of Western civilization was the *wrong* Christianity. The idea that God had become incarnate in Jesus, that his death was an atonement, that he rose from the grave, that he will come again to restore the created order is, in this view, simply false. In fact, the subtitle to *The Jesus Papers* is *Exposing the Greatest Cover-Up in History*.

So, then, what is the truth about Jesus, according to the *Jesus Papers*?

First, Baigent argues that Jesus spent the "silent years," from age twelve to the beginning of his ministry at thirty, in Egypt. Here, for eighteen years, Jesus was under the influence of the religions of Egypt, especially the *Therapeutae*, a mystical religion that affirmed belief in the one divine reality that was never created but was always eternal. The spiritual goal of the *Therapeutae* was to achieve a direct vision of the eternal, the Other, a transcendent experience of the divine, according to Baigent. The message of Jesus was shaped by his spiritual experience in Egypt. His teaching on the kingdom of heaven was simply the message that you can transcend the difficulties of this life and enter into the kingdom of heaven through meditation. Baigent claims the validity of his interpretation on Luke 11:34: "When thine eye is single, thy whole body . . . is full of light" (KJV). Baigent writes, "This is a statement of the purest mysticism worthy of any Buddhist or Taoist from the East. What does Jesus mean by it? In essence, he is saying that if our vision is of the One, then the divine light will embrace us. We will become absorbed into 'God.' "[1]

Baigent not only believes that Jesus taught people how to achieve a transcendent experience, a mystical oneness with the divine Other, he also believes that this message is authenticated as the *secret* that was passed down from Jesus through his apostles and recorded in the Gnostic Gospels. Furthermore, Baigent argues that the church suppressed these documents in order to perpetrate the false teaching of a union of God with Jesus in the incarnation and the subsequent false teaching of his atoning death at the cross and of his resurrection from the dead. Therefore, current Christianity is a false belief, the greatest hoax to appear in world history, argues Baigent.

The hoax began with the Gospels of Matthew, Mark, Luke and John. They do not tell us the truth. These authors, claims Baigent, lied, or their documents were tampered with by the church. Baigent believes that Jesus was put on the cross, but he did not die. The sponge on the hyssop that was put to his mouth had a drug that resulted in the appearance of his death. He was still alive when he was taken down from the cross. His friends carried him to the tomb, where they bathed him with oils, resuscitated him and whisked him and his wife, Mary Magdalene, away.

The only real truth about Jesus is that "he had an experience of the Divine Light that mystics all through the ages reported." The church, on the other hand has, after suppressing the secret Gnostic teaching of Jesus, pushed lies about him ever since. The church has continued to perpetuate such lies, for clearly if the church told the truth about Jesus, it would be finished. "It is really *that* important."[2]

Conclusion

There is a lot of truth to the old adage that history repeats itself. Of course, Christians do not believe in the Greek philosophy of history that sees the recurrence of endless cycles. History, Christians confess, is moving toward its destination in the new heaven and new earth. But the linear view of history does not deny that history, like nature, moves in discernable cycles.

In this chapter I have argued that the history of the Western culture has moved into a cycle of decay. The Christian influence on the Western world has been unraveling for several hundred years and has reached a new low. A crisis is at hand.

> THE COLLAPSE OF
> CHRISTIANITY
> IN THE WESTERN
> WORLD PUTS THE
> WEST INTO A
> VERY VULNERABLE
> POSITION.

One side of this crisis is the world situation of moral decadence, philosophical relativism and religious pluralism. We no longer live in a culture that is narrated by God's involvement in the world through creation, incarnation and re-creation. The ancient religions have made a comeback. True Christianity is under attack, and a false Christianity asserts that Jesus was a guru whose sole mission was to help us escape this world into an experience of light.

The collapse of Christianity in the Western world puts the West into a very vulnerable position. The very foundations of Western civilization shaped by Christian influence have collapsed. It is not enough to say the foundations of Western civilization are endangered. They are already in ruin.

September 11, 2001, is to the Western world what A.D. 410 was to the Roman world. It was two hundred years before Rome was in complete rubble. Today the succession of events happens more rapidly. Western Europe could collapse under Islam in the near future due to its low birth rate and failure to have a comprehensive narrative to withstand the goals of Radical Islam.

America has a stronger political and economic infrastructure, but its moral capacity has been greatly weakened. And similar to Western Europe, the Christian narrative has all but disappeared—the new gnostics have turned Jesus into an Eastern guru and the evangelicals have reduced God's grand narrative of the world into a private narrative that has little or nothing to do with the narrative of the world.

Now, what is happening?

In a world that has no story, new contenders are emerging to narrate the world their way.

Summary

- We now live in a world with no unified narrative, much like the Roman world in which the Christian narrative first appeared.

- Postmodern philosophy celebrates the loss of all narratives and tells us to learn how to live without a universal narrative that gives meaning to life.

- New Age religions, which have swept our secular world, have turned our Western world toward a secular spirituality. They have reenchanted our world with the experience of transcendence—calling us to find our meaning "outside of this world in a religious experience of otherness."

- A popular Gnostic notion of Jesus is that he was a mystic trained in

Egypt—a guru, who like all other mystics calls us to transcend this life and find ourselves united in ecstasy with the light.

- God's narrative for an intentional, obedient and fulfilling respect for human life and sexual relations is a revolutionary message in our lost world.

Recommended Reading

Herrick, James A. *The Making of the New Spirituality: The Eclipse of the Western Religious Tradition*. Downers Grove, Ill.: InterVarsity Press, 2003.

Henderson, David W. *Culture Shift: Communicating God's Truth to Our Changing World*. Grand Rapids: Baker, 1998.

Notes

[1]Michael Baigent, *The Jesus Papers: Exposing the Greatest Cover-Up in History* (San Francisco: HarperSanFrancisco, 2006), p. 236.

[2]Ibid., p. 132.

6

New Contenders Arise
to Narrate the World

Mr. Gorbachev, tear down this wall!"

Most people over thirty will remember these prophetic words spoken by President Reagan in 1987. Little did we realize that these words represented the end of the Cold War and the beginning of a new era.

That new era has been aptly caught by the title of Samuel P. Huntington's book *The Clash of Civilizations and the Remaking of World Order.* The central theme of Huntington's book is that future attempts to narrate the world (though that phrase is not used in his book) will derive not from this or that nation but from civilizations or cultures scattered throughout various nations. Huntington's book is an expansion of an article he wrote in 1993 titled "The Clash of Civilizations." This article was widely read and debated around the world and has turned out to be a prophetic description of the current state of the world.

In brief, Huntington argues that no universal civilization will emerge: Western civilization is in decline; Asian civilizations are expanding; Islam is expanding not only in the East but also in the West; a civilization-based world order is emerging as opposed to the older nation-state world order. Countries are now grouping themselves around the core state of their civilization. The West will increasingly be in conflict with the civilizations grouped around Islam and China, and the survival of the West depends on Americans *reaffirming their Western identity* as unique among the identities of the world and presenting it against the challenges from Islam and a China-based communism.

The question of who gets to narrate the world is not about the changing political scene but rather the demand the new political horizon makes on us spiritually. This clash of civilizations means that we will increasingly experience the clash of the narratives that lie behind the various civilizations. Since these civilizations and the narratives they propose for the world are now no longer geographically contained but are right here at our doorstep, the challenge is to know not only the Christian narrative but the other narratives that seek to explain the world and motivate our actions.

Since this book is primarily about the face off between Islamic and Christian ideology, I will begin with the theological threat of Radical Islam and then proceed to the opposition to Radical Islam from the new secularism and democracy—two other contenders for world rule.

The Threat of Radical Islam for World Domination

Today the most vociferous and violent attempt to narrate the world comes from Radical Islam. It is radically committed to the mandate of Allah to rid the earth of all infidels (non-Muslims) and bring the whole world under Shari'a law.

God. Islam teaches that there is one God who is lord of the universe. (They accuse Christians of polytheism because of the doctrine of the Trinity.) This God is the all-knowing Creator who determines all things. He gives the law, judges people according to their behavior and gives life after death to those who keep his commands. Islam is a system of works—doing Allah's will by keeping the law. As long as a person is obedient to the five pillars of Islam, they are saved and bound for heaven.

Revelation. Allah is a God who reveals. The final and fully authoritative revelations are recorded in the Qur'an, the holy book of Islam. This book is revered by Muslims as the inspired and inerrant written words of

God. A second source of revelation, the Sunna, preserves the words and conduct of Muhammad. These two sources—the Qur'an (God's words) and the Sunna (Muhammad's words)—are the sources for Shari'a, the laws by which one is to live (Shari'a means *the way that leads to God*).

Muhammad. Allah reveals his law through the prophets. The first prophet of Allah is Adam. There are many other prophets as well, including Abraham, Moses, David and Jesus. But the *final* prophet, the one who gives God's completed truth, is Muhammad. Muhammad was born about A.D. 570 and began to receive "revelations" from Allah when he was forty. These revelations occurred primarily in Mecca and Medina (now holy cities) over a period of twenty-two years. Muhammad is not worshiped. Only Allah is worshiped. But the ultimate way to worship Allah is to be obedient to the teachings of Muhammad.

All divisions of Muslims—Sunnis, Shiites and Sufis—follow the Qur'an and the Sunna but are divided over ways of interpretation and application of the laws.

Sunnis. The Sunnis, the largest group of Muslims (approximately 80 percent), reject any interpretation of the Qur'an that is not literal and absolute. And they insist on narrating the world according to a strict interpretation of the Qur'an. Their goal is world domination for the sake of Allah, for Allah is the Lord of the universe who wants the world to live under his law revealed to Muhammad.

Shiites. For those of us who are outsiders to the Muslim community, the differences between the Sunnis and Shiites can be baffling. It is probably similar to the way Muslims view Catholics and Protestants. Shiites and Sunni share the same commitment to Allah, the one true God, to Muhammad as his final prophet and to Shari'a law as the true way of life. Differences include such matters as the Shiite claim that the prophet Ali, who was Muhammad's son-in-law, was the true successor of Muhammad, not Abu Bakr, whom the Sunnis accept. Shiites also reject the Sunni principle of rule through "consensus by community." The Shiites assert that Muhammad directed that Islam be ruled by an imam (spiritual head) who is a direct descendant of Ali. The most famous imam of recent history was Ayatollah (this title means "sign of God") Khomeini (1902-1989) of Iran, who led the revolt against the Shah of Iran in 1979.

Sufis. The Sufis constitute a very small minority of the Muslim population. Unlike the Sunnis and the Shiites, who embrace Islam largely in the external sense, the Sufis seek a close experience of God. They constitute the mystical element of Islam and often attract the New Age crowd looking for a transcendent experience.

Sufism, which has always been a part of Muslim history, insists on the awakening of the heart and an inner experience through an emotional relationship with Allah. One goal of Sufi spirituality is union with Allah. Some Sufi religious leaders have claimed to succeed in merging with Allah. The ritualistic practices of Sufis, which include dancing, singing and chanting, have made them suspect by the Sunnis and the Shiites. In spite of the Sufis' difference with the Sunnis and Shiites, the Sufi influence in the Muslim world is enormous.

> THE FIVE PILLARS
>
> OF ISLAM
>
> Confession
>
> Prayer
>
> Almsgiving
>
> Fasting
>
> Pilgrimage

(Note: Saudi Arabia is predominately Sunni, Iran is predominately Shiite, and the Shiites are the majority in Iraq. Sunnis and Shiites are often at war with each other because of their differing interpretations of the Qur'an and Sunna.)

The five pillars of Islam. What would the world under Allah and Shari'a law look like? For starters, it would be a world under the five pillars of Islam. The first pillar, *Shahada*, is the Muslim confession of faith, which must be said repeatedly throughout the day: "I bear witness that there is no God but Allah, and I bear witness that Muhammad is the messenger of Allah."

The second pillar of Islam is prayer. Prayer, the most important expression of devotion to God, is to occur five times a day. The pray-ers must first prepare for prayer by washing their face, arms, head and feet.

When the crier calls for prayer, Muslims face the holy city of Mecca, raise their hands to their ears and prays "God is greatest." The pray-ers then recite verses from the Qur'an, again saying "God is greatest," while bowing from the waist. Standing in an upright position, the pray-ers say "God is greatest" a third time, then fall to their knees and touch the floor with their forehead. These prayers are obligatory. In the most strict Muslim communities, there are organizations of people who enforce prayer time.

The third pillar of Islam is almsgiving; the fourth, fasting (especially during Ramadan, the month the first verses of the Qur'an were revealed); and the fifth pillar is a pilgrimage to Mecca at least once during the person's lifetime.

Radical Islamists are the fundamentalists who read the Qur'an literally. And there are many injunctions in the Qur'an that clearly teach a militant approach against non-Muslims. Consider these passages:

> Prophet, make war on the unbelievers and the hypocrites and deal rigorously with them. Hell shall be their home: an evil fate. (Surah 9:73)

> Believers, make war on the infidels who dwell around you. Deal firmly with them. Know that God is with the righteous. (Surah 9:123)

> Fight for the cause of God, whether he dies or triumphs, We shall richly reward him. . . . The true believers fight for the cause of God, but the infidels fight for the devil. Fight then against the friends of Satan. . . . Say: "Trifling are the pleasures of this life. The hereafter is better for those who would keep from evil." (Surah 4:74-78)

Radical Islamists who are deeply committed to the teachings of the Qur'an are persuaded that the West is the empire of evil and that God mandates its destruction. Terrorism, which the West sees as an act of evil, is seen by the radical Islamist as a good work of obedience to Allah. Religious violence is thus the way to secure God's reign over all the earth, bringing people under Shari'a law, the only perfect way to God.

Wahhabism. In order to understand the militant emphasis of Islam, one needs to know the influence of Wahhabism, especially among the Sunnis. Wahhabism is not a division of Islam (i.e., Sunnism, Shiism and Sufism). It is instead an emphasis—a strict interpretation of the Qur'an, especially its teaching that all infidels (non-Muslim) and heretical and disobedient Muslims must either follow their strict interpretation of the Qur'an or fall to the sword.

Wahhabism is named after an eighteenth-century Muslim zealot Muhammad ibn Abd al-Wahhab (1703-1792). Wahhab, a student of Islam, argued that the text of the Qur'an must be taken literally and seriously. Wahhab was committed to spreading his message by the sword where necessary. He was particularly focused against the Shiites, convinced that their faith and practice was heretical. His violent crusade against his fellow Muslims was the start of Radical Islam, a phenomena that now reaches around the globe. Of the 1.2 billion Muslims in the world, it is estimated that 25 percent, or approximately 300 million (equal to the population of the United States) are committed to Wahhabism and its goal of bringing the whole world under Allah and Shari'a law. The goal of world dominion will be accomplished through the conversion (or slaughter) of millions. The center from which Wahhabism radiates is Saudi Arabia. This country, rich with oil, has literally poured millions of dollars into founding Wahhabi schools, where children are taught to hate the infidels and commit themselves to become martyrs in the cause of jihad. Saudi Arabia has funded Al-Qaeda, Hezbollah and Hamas with millions of dollars to bring down Western civilization and help to usher in Allah's reign over the whole earth.

Shari'a law. The best way for me to introduce what life under Shari'a law looks like is to turn to the personal account of a young man who embraced Radical Islam but walked away from it through his conversion to the Christian faith.

Daveed Gartenstein-Ross chronicles his spiritual life in *My Year Inside Radical Islam*. By birth Daveed is a Jew. He grew up in Ashland, Oregon, with parents who were not committed to the Jewish faith but

embraced all religions and created their own spiritual path of meditation. When Daveed, a brilliant, well-read student, went to Wake Forest
University in North Carolina, he desired a solid foundation in a particular faith to which he could become committed. He became attracted
to a Muslim student group, which was concerned with issues of social
concern and justice.

Eventually, during a stint of study in Venice, he decided to become a
full-fledged Muslim. On inquiring how he would go about doing this, he
was told that he must make the primary Muslim confession among two
witnesses. That evening among his friends he assented to the two primary
beliefs of Islam, confessing, "I bear witness that there is no object of worship except Allah; and I bear witness that Muhammad is the messenger
of Allah." Daveed took his confession seriously and began immediately to
live in the Muslim way with great enthusiasm and joy.

After graduating from college, he took a job working with a Muslim group. He didn't know that this was a group committed to Radical
Islam. However, almost immediately they required Daveed to submit
to Shari'a law. The first thing Daveed noted was their negative view
toward women, which he rejected. They told him Shari'a law demands
that a man grow a beard because "that's the way God made you" and
"you don't want to look like a woman." He was told "the Prophet . . .
[taught] about everything, down to how you eat your food, and how
you wipe yourself after you go to the bathroom. Islam leaves no room
for question!"[1] Since Daveed was looking for a clear guide for living,
he began to follow all the rules—do not shake hands with a woman;
if you wear shorts they must be below the knee; the lower garment of
your dress must hang to the ankles; never allow your lower garment to
trail on the ground or floor because that is a sign of conceit; touching
or owning dogs is forbidden. Dating is also forbidden. While Daveed
followed all these and other rules, it was the teachings about killing
infidels and heretical Muslims that made him hesitate.

Chief Justice Abdullah bin Muhammad bin Humaid "had argued at
great length that Jihad was not just an acceptable means of establish-

ing an Islamic state, but that *undertaking Jihad was an affirmative duty*."[2]
Daveed, now becoming disillusioned, writes:

> When I became a Muslim I was assured that the progressive vision
> for the faith was the true one, a version of Islam that upheld wom-
> en's rights, human rights, religious freedom, and social justice. A
> version of Islam that was perfectly at peace with all other religions.
> But as I learn more about Islam, I realize that much of what I was
> at first told about it wasn't accurate.[3]

That fall Daveed entered law school and through a renewed friendship
with a high school friend, he began to study the Christian faith. Today, he is
a committed Christian working with the government as a counterterrorism
consultant. The public, he feels, "does not have a good understanding . . .
about the seductive pull of ideology that is today America's deadliest foe."[4]

Contenders Against Radical Islam

Radical Islam is certainly not without its opponents. However, for the most
part, at least at this time, the detractors appear to be lonely voices crying in
the wilderness. There are two contenders that I will mention specifically.
There are certainly more, but these are the opponents that are currently the
most aggressive: the new secular humanism and democracy.

The new secular humanism opposes Radical Islam. The new secularism is best described by Sam Harris in *The End of Faith*. Harris is very
well aware of the current clash of religions (or the clash of narratives). His
answer is to call us to a universal *forsaking of all organized religion*. He
wants us to return to a common universal reason as the only hope for a
world on a collision course over religions. Harris feels certain the world
can come to a new secular and humanistic consensus, and find a universal
spirituality and ethic that transcends religious differences.

Harris levels his argument against religion, not against spirituality.
Religion, as he understands it, is based on the assumption that God has
made a revelation of himself in a book. Religion organizes that revelation
into a set of propositions, a creed, a system of belief, and then its adher-

ents treat their interpretation of the book as truth to be held by everyone. The three religions that are revelation-based are Judaism, Christianity and Islam. We must, he argues, get beyond these religions.

Harris points to all the war and violence that has resulted from the religious convictions that have divided Jews, Christians and Muslims. It is safe to say that these wars have usually been over *land*.

In the medieval age, it was believed that the pope ruled with two arms—one over the church and the other over the state. The church, it was argued, had been given the land of the Roman Empire by the *Donation of Constantine* (which was later exposed as a fake document). Consequently the Christian wars were over the possession of the land, not only in the medieval era, but also in the Reformation era, when Protestants and Catholics fought over control of the land (the Reformers argued that the Bible—not the pope—was over church and state). In the modern world the church is not seen as a landed institution. America and other countries, where there is a strong Christian heritage and influence, are not under the church; the state is sovereign. Though the church may influence the secular state, it does not control the state. Therefore American wars are state wars, not church wars.

On the other hand, the Jews do have a claim to the land of Israel. God promised Abraham, "To your offspring I will give this land" (Gen 12:7). In the Old Testament the Jewish wars all had to do with the possession, repossession and defense of the land. However, the Jews were dispersed throughout the world after being driven from the land by the Romans in A.D. 70. In 1948, after the Holocaust, the Jews were given their land back. For the first time in nearly 1,900 years, the Jews possessed a land they could call their own. The Jewish wars of our time are defensive wars prompted by their belief that this is their land. (Today, most Jews are secular and see the land not as a gift from God but as a result of statehood in 1948. Consequently, they do not consider their wars to be holy wars.)

On the other hand, the radical Islamists believe that God has given them the whole world. Consequently their wars are wars of *conquest*, wars for Allah, who has called them to rule the world.

The point that Harris makes is that religion as a set of beliefs, and especially religion committed to the land, results in violence and war. His point is certainly worth noting.

However, not all of the new secularists repudiate spirituality. The old secularism of the twentieth century was against all transcendence and argued for a world *without* a spiritual consciousness. The new secularism, on the other hand, is a mystical secularism. It follows New Age philosophy—essentially neopaganism, a pantheism that speaks of the spiritual mystery of consciousness at the base of the world. The new secularists believe the only hope for the world is to abandon religion and its truth claims, and turn to the common spirituality of self-consciousness and the ethic of love. In the end the new secularism proclaims the ills of the world will be overcome, when, through the process of evolution, all humans embrace the narrative of self-consciousness and live in the love of divine consciousness.

> PUT ALONGSIDE THE
> ISLAMIC NARRATIVE,
> SECULAR HUMANISM
> WILL COLLAPSE.

But secular humanism—even a spiritual secular humanism—is doomed to failure. The Western world was brought to its present state by secular humanism. Our current moral decay, relativistic philosophy and religious pluralism are the result of secular humanism's rejection of God, revelation and moral absolutes. Secular humanism, far from being our savior, will only deepen the rut into which our society has fallen. Put alongside the Islamic narrative, secular humanism will collapse.

Democracy opposes Radical Islam. Right now there is a significant clash between democracy and Radical Islam. Some see it as a clash of religions. However, the democratic way of life is not tied to the Christian narrative in the same way that the radical Muslim way of life is tied into Islamic theology. Democracy is primarily a political philosophy. The word *democracy* means "rule by the people" and is best described by President Abraham Lincoln as "government of the people, by the people, for the people." The democratic principles of individual freedom and equality are opposed to the radical Islamic principles of religious control of the individual and thus the curtailment of freedom.

In a democracy citizens enjoy protection of their possessions, have equal opportunity to choose and pursue their careers, and do not experience undue interference and control by government. They are free to speak their mind, believe what they wish and behave as they wish within the common laws that govern the land. They can live where they want to live, relocate as they wish and move about freely. They are free to associate with whom they wish, worship at the place of their choice and practice life according to conscience.

Democracy originated in Greece as early as 500 B.C., and its political thinkers criticized all forms of dictatorships. The Romans modified democracy and never practiced it as fully as did the Greeks. Most Roman Emperors were despotic and held the people under a tight reign. In the Middle Ages, following Augustine, Christians believed they were citizens of two kingdoms—the kingdom of God and the kingdom of "men." Unfortunately, when these kingdoms were brought under the authority of the pope, the church and state were inexorably bound together. The Reformation began the process of separating the two kingdoms, and modernity, with the process of secularization, has managed, to a degree, to keep the two separate. Today we speak of a the secular, democratic state and the Christian church as a separate entities. However, we know that church and state are nevertheless intertwined on a broad spectrum— from civil religion on the one hand to the simple but powerful influence of the Christian faith on society on the other hand.

Regardless of how one sees the relationship between Christianity and the political philosophy of democracy, it is clear that Christian principles influenced the development of democratic principles. Democracy is shaped by principles of liberty and equality. We find these principles in democratic documents such as the Magna Carta (1215), the Mayflower Compact (1620), which called for "just and equal laws," and the Declaration of Independence (1776), which state that "all men are created equal. That they are endowed by their creator with certain unalienable rights, that among these are life, liberty and the pursuit of happiness." The Christian principle behind these documents is that of human rights. Certainly it can be said that the dignity of the human person is a direct result of Christian teaching.

Yet the democratic way of narrating the world and the Christian way of narrating the world must not be confused. The terrorists may identify democracy and Christianity as one and the same, but that is a mistake, one that we dare not make. Democracy is a secular form of government strongly influenced by Christian principle. Democracy seeks to narrate a world that is free. Christianity is a faith that narrates the world not through a political philosophy but through the ultimacy of Jesus Christ as Creator and Lord of all history.

> CHRISTIANITY IS A FAITH THAT NARRATES THE WORLD NOT THROUGH A POLITICAL PHILOSOPHY BUT THROUGH THE ULTIMACY OF JESUS CHRIST AS CREATOR AND LORD OF ALL HISTORY.

The ultimate battle that this book addresses is not the political battle between democracy and Islam. Nonetheless, I would quickly affirm the superiority of democracy over Islamic nationalism. Democracy is the most superior form of government devised by humanity, and the goal of establishing democratic rule in Afghanistan, Iraq and other Middle Eastern countries is commendable. It may be difficult to attain, given the resolve, financial backing and fanaticism of Radical Islam, but it is a laudable goal that aims to bring freedom to the oppressed.

Nevertheless, this book is not about the world being narrated by democracy. Democracy may come and go, but what will endure in the struggle with Radical Islam is the unique narrative of the biblical God over against the false narrative of Allah and the misguided efforts of Radical Islam.

Conclusion

In sum, Radical Islam is really the emergence of the older, warlike Islam that sought world control. Like ancient Islam it is convinced it is on a mission to rid the world of all infidels and establish the law of Allah throughout the world.

Radical Islam began with a few followers of Wahhab almost two hundred years ago, but it is now swelling into a tsunami-like wave that is reaching the shores of the Western world. That world was initially shaped by God's narrative but is now reeling under relativism and pluralism, unable to produce a narrative worth living for, let alone dying for.

Radical Islam is faced with two contenders—the new secular humanism and democracy.

The *new secularists* call on us to use our reason and abandon the major religions of the Western world—Jewish, Christian and Muslim. Religion has produced nothing but war and violence. The new secular narrative is based on a spiritual consciousness that will ultimately unite all people in a single common narrative and ethic. But the history of fallen humanity reveals that secularism is doomed to failure.

Through the principles of human rights, freedom and equality, democracy is also a contender to narrate the world. As an American and a beneficiary of democratic rule, there is no question in my mind that the best secular governance of the world is through democratic rule. However, this book is not about a political or economic system—it is about the world being narrated by the triune God of history.

In the final chapter we turn to the challenge of narrating the world once again from the Christian perspective.

Summary

- The clash of civilizations means that we will increasingly experience the clash of narratives that lie behind the various civilizations. The most significant clash now taking place is between the narratives of Christianity and Radical Islam, and it will only grow in the future.

- The Muslim faith is primarily an external faith. It is a faith of obedience and submission to Allah as the one true God, to Muhammad as Allah's final prophet and to Shari'a law as the way of life. The five pillars of Islam constitute the core of that law.

- Wahhabism, whose central location is Saudi Arabia, has generated Radical Islam and is dedicated to the spread of the literal interpretation of the Qur'an and fundamentalist practice of Islam throughout the world.

- Two primary contenders against Radical Islam include the new secular humanism (which is hopeless) and democracy (which Radical Islam opposes vehemently).

- The true hope for the world is to recover the narrative of God, the true narrative of the world.

Recommended Reading

Aslan, Reza. *No God but God: The Origins, Evolution, and Future of Islam*. New York: Random House, 2006.

Gartenstein-Ross, Daveed. *My Year Inside Radical Islam: A Memoir*. New York: Tarcher, 2007.

Harris, Sam. *The End of Faith: Religion, Terror, and the Future of Reason*. New York: W. W. Norton, 2005.

Nafisi, Azar. *Reading Lolita in Tehran: A Memoir in Books*. New York: Random House, 2004.

Notes

[1]Daveed Gartenstein-Ross, *My Year Inside Radical Islam: A Memoir* (New York: Tarcher, 2007), p. 155.

[2]Ibid., p. 190 (emphasis added).

[3]Ibid., p. 238.

[4]Ibid., p. 287.

7

A Call to Narrate the World Christianly

Daveed Gartenstien-Ross, author of *My Year Inside Radical Islam*, was looking for a religion that would provide him a comprehensive worldview—from creation to eschaton. "I believe in God," he would say to himself, "but what is this God like?"

His high school friend pressed him toward the Christian faith, but he kept thinking, *How could a man become God?* He did remember Mike Hollister telling him that he got it wrong—a man didn't become God; God became man.

So, when Daveed came face to face with the nature radical of Islam—its control, legalism, demeaning of women, extreme hate toward all who differ and commitment to kill innocent women and children simply because they were not in submission to Allah—a reappraisal occurred. He had to *compare* Christianity and Islam.

So, he picked up the phone and called his high school buddy Mike Hollister, who immediately sent him a package, including a Bible, a copy of C. S. Lewis's *Mere Christianity* and Josh McDowell's *Evidence That Demands a Verdict*.

His study was thorough, including many conversations, much reading, lots of prayer and thought. He writes, "I thought of the persecution that Jesus' disciples suffered because of their belief in the crucifixion and resurrection. They didn't die for a set of ideals—it was for a set of facts."[1]

Throughout *Who Gets to Narrate the World?* I have not been deal-ing with a myth but with the reality of the God who creates and enters into the time, space and history of the creation he made in order to re-deem, restore and make it new. Yes, Christianity *is* about me, my salva-tion and my relationship to God, but it is also about God's purpose for his creation—a purpose made clear in the Garden. God's purpose for us and for the world, unlike the legalism and judgment of Allah and his prophet Muhammad, is a loving invitation to fellowship and communion with the Father, Son and Holy Spirit, and to a purposeful life of making the world a habitation of his glory. However, we have failed and continue to fail to do God's purpose. So God in Christ has accomplished what we could not do. And God invites us to enter into his narrative by faith and live out his vision of the world.

> GOD INVITES US TO ENTER INTO HIS NARRATIVE BY FAITH AND LIVE OUT HIS VISION OF THE WORLD.

What must we Christians do to narrate this world once again? I sug-gest two urgent commitments: (1) relearn the Christian narrative, and (2) break away from our accommodation to the culture.

Relearn God's Narrative

Christopher Lasch, in his groundbreaking work *The Culture of Nar-cissism*, writes from the perspective that when we lose our connection with the past, there is nothing left to focus on except self. One corrective we must embrace, then, is to return to the origins of God's narrative in Scripture and to the earliest interpretation of it, which was established by the apostles and continued by the ancient church fathers.

For the past thirty years or so the church has been plagued by *inno-vation*. Innovation is the spirit of modernism, a philosophy that moves forward without regard for the past. Modernism assumes that tradition and history are unimportant. American culture is modernist, and unfortunately the American church reflects this spirit in its antihistorical bias and penchant for what's new. The assumption is that new is better.

With an antihistorical attitude and the constant desire for what's new, faith is reduced to *style*. To stay relevant with the changing cultural scene, we must change our style of presenting the faith. Eventually the overemphasis on style results in an underemphasis on substance, and then style overtakes substance. The words of the narrative—*creation, fall, incarnation, death, resurrection, second coming*—may continue to be used, but without the appropriate depth and cosmic substance. And that is why there is a need to stay connected to the tradition.

The word *tradition* is unpopular in American evangelicalism. Yet it is found in the New Testament. Paul points to Jesus' fulfillment of history in his death and resurrection as the *tradition* of the church. He tells the Corinthians that this tradition was passed down to him, that he reveres this tradition and that he has now passed it down to them. They too are to revere it and pass it on to others (1 Cor 15:1-6).

God's narrative of the world—the traditional foundation of the church—is held dear by every Christian body. It is the common narrative of Catholics, Orthodox and Protestants. However, as it has been passed down in history it gathers traditions around it. So we all have our additional traditions: Orthodox have icons, Catholics have the pope and Mary, and the various Protestant groups have traditions that distinguishes them from each other. Unfortunately we often emphasize how and why we differ and even fight over those differences.

However, given the world situation and the new anti-Christian contenders to the narration of the world—especially Radical Islam—it is urgent that we come together. I don't mean in an organized, institutional way, but spiritually, through our common tradition: God's narrative.

But God's narrative must not be blithely recited as a litany of words. We must recover the profound original interpretation of God's narrative—that of the early church. They handed down to us in tradition the canon of Scripture, the great ecumenical creeds, the liturgies, the catechumenate and the ethics of faith. By recovering this ancient narrative, we will be able to speak once again to the world about its own history, telling the truth about the triune God who creates and who becomes involved in his own creation to restore it.

A Call to an Ancient Evangelical Future

Much of what I am writing about in this book—recovering the narrative of God—has been at the forefront of my heart and mind for a number of years. My initial impetus toward relearning God's narrative took shape as a response to the postmodern rejection of all universal narratives (or metanarratives). As I became more and more conscious of the rejection of metanarratives, I became more keenly aware that this is exactly what the Christian message is—a single, universal narrative of everything.

Then, as Radical Islam began to dominate world news, I saw the contest emerge between two very different world narratives. I became persuaded more than ever that we Christians must stop building our case for Christianity around modern science and reason, and return to the ancient way of approaching God's truth as the narrative of the world.

In the fall of 2006 I asked my colleague Phil Kenyon, director of the Grow Center for Biblical Leadership at Northern Seminary, to join me in writing "A Call to an Ancient Evangelical Future." This call was written by us through e-mail correspondence with a community of Christian scholars and practitioners over a period of seven months. The call basically bids Christians to return to God's narrative of the world. Rather than write something new I offer this call as a challenge to recover the narrative nature of God's Word so that we may be prepared to address the most pressing spiritual issue of our time:

Prologue
In every age the Holy Spirit calls the church to examine its faithfulness to God's revelation in Jesus Christ, authoritatively recorded in Scripture and handed down through the church. Thus, while we affirm the global strength and vitality of worldwide evangelical-

ism in our day, we believe the North American expression of evangelicalism needs to be especially sensitive to the new external and internal challenges facing God's people.

These external challenges include the current cultural milieu and the resurgence of religious and political ideologies. The internal challenges include evangelical accommodation to civil religion, rationalism, privatism and pragmatism. In light of these challenges, we call evangelicals to strengthen their witness through a recovery of the faith articulated by the consensus of the ancient church and its guardians in the traditions of Eastern Orthodoxy, Roman Catholicism, the Protestant Reformation and the evangelical awakenings. Ancient Christians faced a world of paganism, Gnosticism and political domination. In the face of heresy and persecution, they understood history through Israel's story, culminating in the death and resurrection of Jesus and the coming of God's kingdom.

Today, as in the ancient era, the church is confronted by a host of master narratives that contradict and compete with the gospel. The pressing question is: Who gets to narrate the world? The "Call to an Ancient Evangelical Future" challenges evangelical Christians to restore the priority of the divinely inspired biblical story of God's acts in history. The narrative of God's kingdom holds eternal implications for the mission of the church, its theological reflection, its public ministries of worship and spirituality and its life in the world. By engaging these themes, we believe the church will be strengthened to address the issues of our day.

On the Primacy of the Biblical Narrative

We call for a return to the priority of the divinely authorized canonical story of the triune God. This story—creation, incarnation and re-creation—was effected by Christ's recapitulation of human history and summarized by the early church in its rules of faith. The gospel-formed content of these rules served as the key to the interpretation of Scripture and its critique of contemporary culture, and thus shaped the church's pastoral ministry. Today, we call evangelicals to turn away from modern theological methods that reduce the gospel to mere propositions, and from contemporary pastoral ministries so compatible with culture that they camouflage God's story or empty it of its cosmic and redemptive meaning. In a world of competing stories, we call evangelicals to recover the truth of God's Word as *the* story of the world, and to make *it* the centerpiece of evangelical life.

On the Church, the Continuation of God's Narrative

We call evangelicals to take seriously the visible character of the church. We call for a commitment to its mission in the world in fidelity to God's mission (*missio Dei*), and for an exploration of the ecumenical implications this has for the unity, holiness, catholicity and apostolicity of the church. Thus, we call evangelicals to turn away from an individualism that makes the church a mere addendum to God's redemptive plan. Individualistic evangelicalism has contributed to the current problems of churchless Christianity, redefinitions of the church according to business models, separatist ecclesiologies and judgmental attitudes toward the church. Therefore, we call evangelicals to recover their place in the community of the church catholic.

On the Church's Theological Reflection on God's Narrative

We call for the church's reflection to remain anchored in the Scriptures in continuity with the theological interpretation learned from the early fathers. Thus, we call evangelicals to turn away from methods that separate theological reflection from the common traditions of the church. These modern methods compartmentalize God's story by analyzing its separate parts, while ignoring God's entire redemptive work as recapitulated in Christ. Antihistorical attitudes also disregard the common biblical and theological legacy of the ancient church.

Such disregard ignores the hermeneutical value of the church's ecumenical creeds. This reduces God's story of the world to one of many competing theologies and impairs the unified witness of the church to God's plan for the history of the world. Therefore, we call evangelicals to unity in "the tradition that has been believed everywhere, always and by all," as well as to humility and charity in their various Protestant traditions.

On the Church's Worship as Telling and Enacting God's Narrative

We call for public worship that sings, preaches and enacts God's story. We call for a renewed consideration of how God ministers to us in baptism, Eucharist, confession, the laying on of hands, marriage, healing and through the charisma of the Spirit, for these actions shape our lives and signify the meaning of the world. Thus, we call evangelicals to turn away from forms of worship that focus on God as a mere object of the intellect or that assert the self as the source of worship. Such worship has resulted in lecture-oriented, music-driven, performance-centered and program-controlled models that do not adequately proclaim God's cosmic redemption. Therefore, we call evangelicals to recover the historic substance of worship of Word and Table and to attend to the Christian year, which marks time according to God's saving acts.

On Spiritual Formation in the Church as Embodiment of God's Narrative

We call for a catechetical spiritual formation of the people of God that is based firmly on a trinitarian biblical narrative. We are concerned when spirituality is separated from the story of God and baptism into the life of Christ and his body. Spirituality, made independent from God's story, is often characterized by legalism, mere intellectual knowledge, an overly therapeutic culture, New Age gnosticism, a dualistic rejection of this world and a narcissistic preoccupation with one's own experience. These false spiritualities are inadequate for the challenges we face in today's world. There-

fore, we call evangelicals to return to a historic spirituality like that
taught and practiced in the ancient catechumenate.

On the Church's Embodied Life in the World

We call for a cruciform holiness and commitment to God's mission in the world. This embodied holiness affirms life, biblical morality and appropriate self-denial. It calls us to be faithful stewards
of the created order and bold prophets to our contemporary culture. Thus, we call evangelicals to intensify their prophetic voice
against forms of indifference to God's gift of life, economic and
political injustice, ecological insensitivity and the failure to cham-
pion the poor and marginalized. Too often we have failed to stand
prophetically against the culture's captivity to racism, consumerism, political correctness, civil religion, sexism, ethical relativism,
violence and the culture of death. These failures have muted the
voice of Christ to the world through his church and detract from
God's story of the world, which the church is collectively to embody. Therefore, we call the church to recover its countercultural
mission to the world.

Epilogue

In sum, we call evangelicals to recover the conviction that God's
story shapes the mission of the church to bear witness to God's
kingdom and to inform the spiritual foundations of civilization.
We set forth this call as an ongoing, open-ended conversation. We
are aware that we have our blind spots and weaknesses. Therefore,
we encourage evangelicals to engage this call within educational
centers, denominations and local churches through publications
and conferences.

We pray that we can move with intention to proclaim a loving,
transcendent, triune God who has become involved in our history.
In line with Scripture, creed and tradition, it is our deepest desire
to embody God's purposes in the mission of the church through

our theological reflection, our worship, our spirituality and our life in the world, all the while proclaiming that Jesus is Lord over all creation.[2]

How God's Narrative Shapes the Church and Its Ministries

The major goal of the "Call to an Ancient Evangelical Future" was to re-present the priority of the narrative of God and to show how God's narrative is the subject of the church and its ministries. *Everything that the church is and does flows out of God's narrative.*

There is an urgent need to restore this connection between the narrative, the church and its ministries. It is urgent because the church and its ministries are currently disconnected from the narrative. Leaders are confused about the topics the call addresses:

- What is God's narrative?

- What is the church?

- What is theology?

- What is worship?

- What is spirituality?

- What is the life of the church in the world?

Here is the issue: When the church and its ministries are disconnected from God's narrative, they become subject to the whims of culture. So who then gets to define the church and its ministries? Culture? Philosophy? Sociology? Anthropology? Politics? Business? Marketing? Consumerism? The media?

I hope you see what I mean. Let me spell it out more clearly by summarizing how people who have been overly influenced by current cultural ideology think of the church and its ministries apart from its source in God's narrative.

- The *church* has become a business that sells Jesus—the culture of consumerism.

- *Theology* has become an analytical discipline that scientifically examines propositions—the culture of reason.

- *Worship* has become an entertaining program that presents Jesus in a winsome way—the culture of entertainment.

- *Spirituality* has become an experience of transcendence achieved through Christian technique—the New Age culture of generic spirituality.

- *The church's life in the world* is to do good so people can see that Jesus is all about being nice and helpful—the culture of humanism.

- But all this changes when we resituate the church and its ministries within God's narrative. The "Call to an Ancient Evangelical Future" spells this out in a little more detail, but let me give you the sense of the church and its ministries formed by God's narrative in the following summaries:

- God's *narrative* is the one true story of the world.

- The church's *mission* is to be a witness to God's narrative of the world *(missio Dei).*

- *Theology* is the church's corporate reflection on God's narrative.

- *Worship* sings, proclaims and enacts God's narrative to the glory of God.

- Individual *spirituality* is the personal embodiment of God's narrative in all of life.

- Collective *spirituality* is the church's embodied life in the world.

These brief summaries point to the relationship between God's narrative of the world, the church and its ministries. It is crucial that God's narrative and Christian practice be brought back together, because the ministries of the church are currently separated from the narrative and shaped by forces other than God's narrative.

By entering deeply into the recovery of God's cosmic story, we will be able to deal personally with the ideological battle posed by those who contend for the narration of our world. We will increasingly learn how to live out of God's narrative, to see the world and current events through

God's eyes and, if need be, stand faithful unto the death in the truth of God's narrative.

However, there are, as I have indicated throughout this work, ways in which God's narrative has become altered through cultural accommodation. Therefore, in addition to relearning God's narrative in the face of the spiritual struggle with Radical Islam, *we must unlearn and unravel the cultural accommodations embraced by the church* in order

> WHEN THE CHURCH
> AND ITS MINISTRIES
> ARE DISCONNECTED
> FROM GOD'S NARRATIVE,
> THEY BECOME SUBJECT
> TO THE WHIMS
> OF CULTURE.

to release the full power and impact of God's full narrative, not only for the benefit of individuals but also for the benefit of society and civilization, especially the collapsing world of the West.

Reform Our Accommodation to the Cultural Milieu

In my association with many who affirm the faith—students, pastors, laypeople—I find that, though the words of the Christian narrative are recited, the profound meaning and depth of the narrative have suffered a considerable reduction. These reductions occurred through a Christianity tainted by civil religion, rationalism, privatism and pragmatism. A brief review of each of these issues will help us understand where the surgeon's knife needs to be applied to regain the health of the Christian narrative.

Do not accommodate God's narrative to civil religion. Jean-Jacques Rousseau (1712-1778) was the first person to use the term *civil religion*. He attempted to resolve the problem of the tension between religion and culture in a pluralistic society by speaking of a "social contract." He recognized that no state could exist without having some kind of religion at its base. But he chided Christianity because he felt that it weakened the state by setting forth a dual allegiance for believers. He sought to solve this problem through the creation of a civil religion, which he identified as "a purely civil profession of faith." This would provide the "social sentiments without which a person cannot be a good citizen or a faithful subject." He insisted that these sentiments should be "few, simple, and exactly worded" and suggested they include "the existence of a mighty, intelligent, and beneficent Divinity possessed of foresight and providence, the life to come, the happiness of the just, the punishment of the wicked, the sanctity of the social contract and the laws."[3] In other words, he saw religion as the moral glue that held society together. It was the will of the people expressed religiously within the state so that the state assumes a religious character. This is civil religion.

The roots of American civil religion go back to England and its self-concept as a "chosen nation." This idea was popularized by John Foxe (1517-1587) in his widely read *Book of Martyrs*. Foxe set forth the story of suffering Protestants in such a way as to make England appear to be especially called by God to retain and spread the truth. England was God's chosen nation, and through it the divine plan of God would be fulfilled.

The Puritans brought this idea of an elect nation to America. The hope of a new people of God is clearly seen in the famous words of John Winthrop (1588-1649):

> Wee shall finde that the God of Israell is among us, when tenn of us shall be able to resist a thousand of our enemies, when hee shall make us a prayse and glory, that men shall say of succeeding plantacions; the Lord make it like that of New England: for wee must consider that wee shall be as a citty upon a Hill, the eies of all people are upon us.[4]

During the eighteenth-century Great Awakening, the idea that America was a chosen nation was further strengthened by the preaching and influence of Jonathan Edwards (1703-1758). He encouraged people to gather for prayers for the coming of God's kingdom. It was his conviction that the millennium, the thousand-year reign of Christ on earth, might come to America. Other revivalists picked up this theme, and through them a sense of special destiny was instilled in the American soul.

This sense was heightened through the American Revolution. Politicians and preachers alike compared the American situation to Israel and the exodus. The British were the Egyptians in hot pursuit of America, the new Israel. But God was on the American side, just as he was on Israel's, and he would see America through its Red Sea and then through the wilderness to the Promised Land.

In the nineteenth century most evangelical preachers and leaders thought the millennium would come as a result of the Christianization of the world. The great revivalists, such as Lyman Beecher (1775-1863) and Charles G. Finney (1792-1875), were convinced that God had chosen America to lead the way in the moral and political emancipation of the world. It was America's destiny to prepare the world for the coming of Christ.

Gradually, Protestants began to see the nation as the means through which God was working in history. The concept of a chosen people became that of a chosen nation. Against this background the role of Christians in the spread of American imperialism is understandable. Spreading of Americanism was equal to spreading Christianity, for in the American character one could most clearly see the character of God. Consequently an American messianic consciousness emerged; it was believed that America would deliver the world from its woes.[5]

This issue of a civil religion is still with us today. Some view America as a Christian nation that stands against radical Muslims, who constitute an Islamic nation. However, the current military face off with Islam is not the Christian narrative against the Islamic narrative. Democracy, which is in conflict with Radical Islam, is a secular form of government *influenced* by the Christian narrative. Therefore, it is perfectly appropriate for Christians to support America's agenda to form democratic states within the context of totalitarian states. A democratic state supports human rights. Where democracy exists, women are treated better, laws are more just, the freedom of the individual is supported, and free enterprise flourishes. A Christian can be a patriot and support democracy and its spread around the world as the best of the secular narratives. How could anyone argue the case that Radical Islam or communism or socialism is a better way to govern and live?

But just because democracy is influenced by the implications of Christian narrative does not make it the Christian narrative. The Christian narrative is God's story of the world, and throughout history God's people have lived in God's narrative under the authority of every conceivable political and economic system devised by the world.

> IF WE ARE TO RECOVER THE CHRISTIAN NARRATIVE, WE MUST FIRST DISABUSE OURSELVES OF CIVIL RELIGION.

So if we are to recover the Christian narrative, we must first disabuse ourselves of civil religion. We live in two narratives simultaneously. We live in the narrative of God *and* within a culture that lives by the narrative of democracy. The two narratives are separate, yet we live in them both simultaneously. However, as Christians, our ultimate commitment is to God's narrative: "Jesus is Lord." There is no other worthy allegiance.

Do not accommodate God's narrative to rationalism. We are not going to be able to recover the narrative nature of the Christian faith until we get past our dependence on human reason and science to prove the faith. Neither the ancient church fathers nor the Reformers looked to reason as the foundations of the Christian faith. For them the narrative of God's activity in history stood on its own. Instead of bringing reason to the narrative as a way of shoring it up and making it acceptable, they asked us to live in the narrative and interpret philosophy and all other disciplines from within the narrative. Anselm of Canterbury (1033-1109) famously referred to this posture as "faith seeking understanding." The issue is this: Are you aligned with the world's way of thinking and judge the Christian faith, or do you stand in the Christian faith and see the world through God's narrative?

Narrative thinking *reverses* the world's way of doing things. Let me give you an example. Several years ago I was invited to debate an atheist philosopher on a popular Midwest radio show. The host began by asking the philosopher to state his argument against God. His arguments were clear, cogent and quite persuasive. Then the host turned to me. "Bob, how do you answer him?" What the host was looking for was a debate based on reason, logic and evidence.

"His arguments are great," I said. "I don't plan to engage any of them; it would be futile. I can't really argue effectively *for* God's existence any more than he can argue effectively *against* God's existence on the basis of reason. The debate rests on perspective, not reason. So, no, I can't engage what he just said."

Shocked, the host responded, "Bob, we have a two-hour show! What are we going to talk about?

"Well," I said, "why don't we explore the narrative of Israel, Jesus and the church, and ask ourselves what this narrative says about a God who becomes involved in history?"

For two hours we discussed the exodus event, Israel and its relation to the Christ event, the church, the purposes of life, and the destiny of history. It was a *good* conversation—full of life, energy and provocative thought. The idea of proving God's existence was not even raised. But the profundity of God's narrative was explored and became quite evident even in expressions of wonder.

At the end of the show, as I was leaving the studio, the atheist philosopher said, "Bob, have you got a minute? You know," he said, "this conversation affected me deeply. I didn't admit it during the show, but I am a Jew. We keep a kosher home, and we observe the sabbath and the festivals. It never occurred to me that the narrative itself, in which I participate, is a witness to God. This discussion has given me a lot to think about."

The point I want to make is that we must stop standing outside the narrative and judging it by human reason or any other intellectual discipline. Such an approach makes God and God's narrative an object of investigation. We become the arbiter of its truthfulness.

Instead, we must stand *inside* the narrative. God is not an object within the narrative. When we stand inside the narrative by faith, we stand under, not over, him, and we see the world through the narrative, not the other way around.

> WE MUST
>
> STAND *INSIDE*
>
> THE NARRATIVE.

This is why I say we must get past rationalism. As long as we stand outside God's narrative and judge it through reason—that is, *human* reason—we will never be able to see the world as God sees it. The world, then, will only be shaped by God's narrative when we stand inside that narrative— preaching, worshiping, ministering, acting from within.

Do not accommodate God's narrative to privatism and consumerism. The narrative of God has both a universal cosmic scope and a private dimension. Paul frequently speaks of both. Christ is the Creator and Redeemer of all things, visible and invisible (Col 1:13-22), and he is the One who lives in me (Gal 2:20).

We dare not lose either the cosmic or the personal dimensions of God's narrative. Those who lose the personal dimension lose a relationship with the divine, which is based on God's work in Christ for us. In the incarnation God unites with our humanity. He cancels the debt of sin at the cross, defeats the death under which we live and frees us from our enslavement to sin so that we can live a new life in his resurrection. Personal spirituality is grounded in God's work in Christ.

However, this work, personal as it is, is also cosmic. In his incarnation, death and resurrection, Christ defeats the powers of evil that from the Fall have sought to deface God's creation by turning humanity away from God's purposes in history. Because of evil all God's creation lies under bondage to decay. Death to God's purposes extends into the political, economic, institutional, ideological, familial and relational dimensions of life. By his death and resurrection, Jesus Christ sets all creation free. Now creation itself is pregnant with its own redemption, awaiting the day of the coming again when God's work in history will be finally consummated.

Privatism, which is a preoccupation with God's narrative for *me*, forgets the cosmic nature of God's narrative and results in a narcissistic faith. Narcissism, the focus on the self, is a cultural phenomenon that began in the 1970s and continues to this day. Through marketing, narcissism has been extended into every aspect of our culture.

The Western economy shifted from selling products to selling an experience. What sells a product is not its substance, but *what it will do for me*. It supposedly makes my life more meaningful, more exciting, more attractive. Unfortunately, the Christian faith, following the curvature of culture, began to be packaged as an experience to sell to the consumer. Narcissistic faith lost its substance— the cosmic narrative of God—and was presented as a consumer experience. The faith will give me meaning, make life more full, solve my problems.

> PRIVATISM . . . FORGETS THE COSMIC NATURE OF GOD'S NARRATIVE.

Churches embrace this narcissistic approach to life when they shape ministry by need. Find out, we are told, what people are looking for, and provide it for them. Consequently the church as a living witness to God's narrative became the place where the consumer could buy a product that fulfilled his or her needs. Of course, the church does fulfill needs, but they must be placed within the cosmic narrative, thereby reducing the individual's focus on self and turning his or her contemplation to God's saving deeds, whereby the whole world is made right.

The same has also happened to the church's worship and spirituality. Worship has become narcissistic, focusing on *me* and *my* praise of God; and spirituality has turned toward a preoccupation with *my* journey of faith and *my* spiritual condition and experience.

There is of course an appropriate place for my worship and spirituality, but when we become narcissistic, the place of worship and spirituality in God's narrative is lost and worship and spirituality become subject to the whims of culture.

So, to narrate the world we must become conscious of how our privatized approach to the church, its worship and its spirituality have prevented the Christian narrative from influencing the way we think about life in the world.

Do not accommodate God's narrative to pragmatism. Another menace that lurks at the door of the Christian narrative is pragmatism. Pragmatism always asks, Does it work? Does it produce? Is it effective? Pragmatism has moved the church toward a business model. This follows, of course, the consumer approach to the faith. Jesus becomes the product marketed to people—the consumers—to satisfy their needs. The pastor then becomes the CEO, and the church is run according to the principles of the Fortune 500 companies. The focus is on buildings, programs and outcomes. Primary attention is given to technique, to efficiency and production.

It is difficult to criticize pragmatism, because it has resulted in the megachurch movement where many needs have been met and many lives have been transformed. My concern here is not to demean these results but to point to the ways that an overemphasis on pragmatism has led to the loss of God's narrative for the world. I'm calling not for the tearing down of the megachurch but for the recovery of God's narrative and for the role the church plays as the witness to God's narrative.

Conclusion

If we are to narrate the world once again by God's story, then the church, theological reflection, worship, spirituality and our life in the world must be returned to God's narrative and reformed by the story of what God is doing in the world. Furthermore, we must unlearn the ways that the ministries of the church have been corrupted by cultural accommodation—civil religion, rationalism, privatism, consumerism and pragmatism.

We live in a crucial time of history, a time when our faith will be increasingly tested by the enemies of God's true narrative. The powers and principalities still actively oppose the Lord of history and seek to distort and destroy his truth. *Who gets to narrate the world?* is not a mere academic question. If Christians are to witness to God's mission to restore the world, to recover the Garden, to establish once again the communion of God's creatures within the communion and fellowship of the triune God, then we must know the narrative, proclaim it and live it—to the death if necessary.

Surely, this is the most pressing issue of our time.

Summary

- God's narrative must not be blithely recited as a litany of words. Rather we must recover the profound original interpretation of God's narrative—that interpretation made by the early church.

- If we recover this ancient narrative, we will once again be able to speak to the world about its own history and tell the truth about the triune God, who creates and becomes involved in his own creation to restore it as his eternal Garden and people.

- God's narrative is the subject of the church and its ministries. Everything that the church is and does flow out of God's narrative. Therefore there is an urgent need to restore this connection between the narrative, the church and its ministries.

- We must unlearn and unravel the cultural accommodations embraced by the church in order to release the full power and impact of God's narrative, not only for the benefit of humanity but also for the welfare of society and civilization, especially the collapsing world of the West.

Recommended Reading

Bartholomew, Craig, and Michael W. Goheen. *The Drama of Scripture: Finding Our Place in the Biblical Story*. Grand Rapids: Baker, 2004.

Hart, David Bentley. *The Beauty of the Infinite: The Aesthetics of Christian Truth*. Grand Rapids: Eerdmans, 2003.

Lee, Philip J. *Against the Protestant Gnostics*. New York: Oxford University Press, 1987.

Vanhoozer, Kevin J. *The Drama of Doctrine. A Canonical Linguistic Approach to Christian Doctrine.* Louisville: Westminster John Knox Press, 2005.

Notes

[1]Daveed Gartenstein-Ross, *My Year Inside Radical Islam: A Memoir* (New York: Tarcher, 2007), p. 133.

[2]Robert Webber and Phil Kenyon, "A Call to an Ancient Evangelical Future," Northern Seminary, 2006. This Call is issued in the spirit of *sic et non*; therefore those who affix their names to this call need not agree with all its content. Rather, its consensus is that these are issues to be discussed in the tradition of *semper reformanda* as the church faces the new challenges of our time. Over a period of seven months, more than three hundred persons participated via e-mail to write the Call. These men and women represent a broad diversity of ethnicity and denominational affiliation. The four theologians who most consistently interacted with the development of the Call have been named the "theological editors." The board of reference was given the special assignment of overall approval. Permission is granted to reproduce the Call in unaltered form with proper citation. To sign the Call go to www.ancientfutureworship.com.

[3]Jean-Jacques Rousseau, *The Social Contract and Discourses*, trans. and ed. G. D. H. Cole (New York: Dutton, 1950), p. 139.

[4]John Winthrop, "A Model of Christian Charity," in H. S. Smith, R. T. Handy and Lefferts A. Loetscher, *American Christianity: An Historical Interpretation with Representative Documents* (New York: Scribner, 1960), 1:102.

[5]The material on civil religion was adapted from Robert E. Webber, *The Secular Saint* (Grand Rapids: Zondervan, 1979), pp. 128-32.

Conclusion

A Challenge

In *Who Gets to Narrate the World?* I have sounded a wake-up call—a call to all Christians to become aware of the most pressing spiritual issue of our time. The issue has two parts, external and internal. The external threat is the spiritual struggle against the worldwide domination of Radical Islam. The internal threat is the spiritual struggle against the forces of American consumerism and privatism that seek to undermine the primacy of God's narrative.

Many Christians and non-Christians in America do not think deeply about these questions. They read of what is going on in the Middle East and in Europe but appear to be impervious to the threat reaching the shores of North America. And they see the moral and spiritual decay in the Western culture that surrounds them but think they aren't affected by it. But we must *wake up*, for the satanic forces are mounting and the threat to the church and to Western society is more real than most suspect.

What I have offered in this book is a postmodern apologetic—an ancient way of understanding and presenting the Christian faith—a comprehensive narrative of the world. I have set forth this apologetic first of all to strengthen *you*, the Christian, for what lies ahead. Second, should you have an opportunity to witness to a Muslim, this book should help you to be better prepared. My approach is simple, involving three imperatives.

First, we need knowledge of the biblical-theological narrative. The modern apologetic uses reason, science and other disciplines to prove the accuracy and superiority of God's narrative. The postmodern apologetic, which looks back to the apostles and the apostolic tradition developed by the ancient fathers, simply tells the story. The comprehensive story of God is a story that *stands on its own* and does not need external support. The heart of the story is how God became one of us to take our suffering into himself, to deal with sin, overcome death, and to be resurrected to new life—all in order that fallen creation could be restored to right relationship with God.

Islam has no such story. It has only one way to deal with sin—obey; keep the rules. It has only one way to deal with death—to pass through it. Take time to make a comparison between the faith of Islam and Christianity. *Know God's narrative.* To do so, we have to take an ax to the way the Christian faith has accommodated to culture. Become increasingly aware of how our Christianity has been reduced to my private narrative, and how it has been corrupted by civil religion, rationalism and pragmatism. These two sides of defense—recovering the biblical-theological narrative and turning away from Christian accommodation to culture— are huge expectations, but they are absolutely necessary for the faithful narration of the world and the defense of human freedom in the twenty-first century.

The second imperative is to recover the historical trajectory of the church. I am not suggesting that you memorize all the details of church history, but that you understand the narrative of the Western church, our heritage. I have outlined that heritage in this book, showing how Christianity originated in pagan Rome, how it witnesses and lived in a world of moral decadence, philosophical relativism and religious pluralism. I then briefly spoke of the influence the faith had on the foundations of the Western civilization. This information is good to know, especially when you encounter someone who discounts Christianity as an oppressive, warlike faith. History also reveals how the church thrived under persecution, how it was compromised by culture, and how, when Christian witness was at an all time low, it was revived in new ways.

Third, we must take into account the contemporary situation we find ourselves in. We can more effectively bring the biblical-theological narrative to our present situation when we know where we are and how we got here. For this reason it is important to know the history of how God's world-encompassing narrative was reduced to a private matter by the rise of secularism. Secularism has won on three accounts—(1) by challenging the cosmic dimension of the gospel, (2) by forcing Christians to reducing the gospel to our personal journey, and (3) by inducing Christians to defend the gospel by means of reason and science. The testimony to the truth of God's narrative is not found outside but inside the Bible, in its story, its symbols and its prophecies. There is no narrative that begins to compare with the Christian narrative—in which God enters our suffering to deliver us from sin and death, and to deliver the world from the domain of darkness.

It doesn't get any better than that!

Allah is not Lord. Shari'a law is not what we are called to live under.

You are not the lord of your own, self-oriented life.

Jesus is Lord! And this truth will make you free.

269
W372

119386

LINCOLN CHRISTIAN COLLEGE AND SEMINARY

3 4711 00182 3964